THE BEST OF
GLACIER
NATIONAL PARK

by ALAN LEFTRIDGE

FARCOUNTRY
PRESS

*Glacier National Park's mascot enjoys the view at Hidden Lake Overlook.
(Goats often lick handrails for the salt residue.)*

THE BEST OF
GLACIER
NATIONAL PARK

by ALAN LEFTRIDGE

ISBN: 978-1-56037-560-9

For more information on our books, write Farcountry Press, P.O. Box 5630,
Helena, MT 59604; call (800) 821-3874; or visit www.farcountrypress.com.

Library of Congress Cataloging-in-Publication Data

Leftridge, Alan.
  Best of Glacier National Park / by Alan Leftridge.
     pages cm
  ISBN-13: 978-1-56037-560-9 (13)
  ISBN-10: 1-56037-560-4 (10)
  1. Glacier National Park (Mont.)–Guidebooks. I. Title.
  F737.G5L43 2013
  978.6'52–dc23

                                              2013002917

 Produced and printed in the United States of America.

19 18 17 16 15   2 3 4 5 6

TABLE OF CONTENTS

PREFACE

"We're here! What should we do, what is there to see?"

As a park ranger, I heard this exclamation and question many times, as family members would approach me in the visitor center. Excited to be at their vacation destination, they wanted to start making memories. The pleasure expressed in their eyes when they heard about the fun things awaiting them was my lasting reward.

My first visit to a national park was a vacation to Rocky Mountain National Park in Colorado. I was eight. I recall a flood of feelings, from excitement to a great calm, and also a burning curiosity. As an adult, I have lived in and worked near Yellowstone, Redwood, and Glacier national parks. My work has taken me to many other national parks. I have come to understand that the collection of emotions always includes excitement, a sense of wonder, a state of serenity, and reflection.

"What should we do, what is there to see?" is a great question to ask a park employee, or a friend. But what if neither is available, as you make your plans for your visit?

The purpose of this book is to highlight the iconic features of Glacier National Park, and Waterton Lakes National Park in Canada, and to share with you the Best of Glacier as identified by the people who work and live here. I'm happy to share with you what you should know about Glacier, as if you were a family member or friend visiting the park for the first time.

So, this book is for you. To encourage you to experience the excitement, wonder, serenity, and opportunities for reflection that can be found in Glacier, through sightseeing, hiking, wildlife viewing, wildflower admiration, painting, photographing, and learning its natural and cultural history. These stories and experiences will lead you to the heart and soul of the Crown of the Continent.

Alan Leftridge
Swan Valley, Montana

HOW TO USE THE MAPS IN THIS BOOK

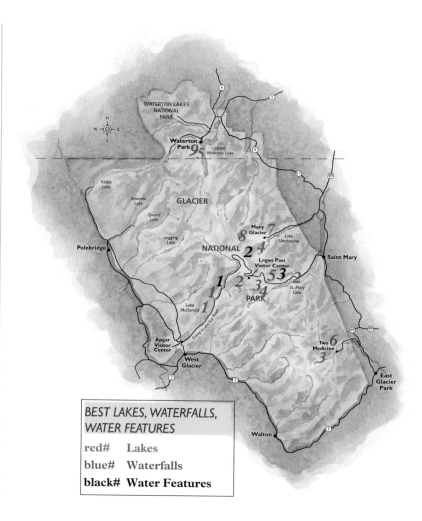

BEST LAKES, WATERFALLS, WATER FEATURES

red#   Lakes
blue#   Waterfalls
black#   Water Features

The maps in this book show locations for features described in each chapter. Some indicate general areas where plants or animals may be observed. Other maps indicate more specific locations with numbers that correspond to the text. A few maps (such as the example on this page) show multiple features with color coding explained in a legend below the map.

GLACIER NATIONAL PARK FAST FACTS

- Glacier National Park was established in 1910.
- Annual visitation exceeds 2 million.
- The park's land area is 1,013,594 acres, or 1,583 square miles.
- The Going-to-the-Sun Road took over 10 years to complete. The road opened in 1933.
- There are 37 named glaciers.
- The largest glacier is Blackfoot Glacier at 423 acres.
- Glacier National Park's low point is 3,150 feet at the confluence of the Middle and North Forks of the Flathead River.
- Glacier has 175 mountains.
- Six mountains are more than 10,000 feet in elevation.
- Mount Cleveland is the highest point at 10,466 feet.
- The Continental Divide runs through the park for 106 miles.
- At Triple Divide Peak, a raindrop could end up in the Gulf of Mexico, Pacific Ocean, or Hudson Bay. This is the only place in the United States that is a headwaters to three oceans— Atlantic, Pacific, and Arctic.
- The park is home to more than 1,400 species of plants, 25 species of trees, 277 species of birds, 68 species of mammals, and 24 species of fish.
- There are 151 maintained trails in Glacier National Park, totaling 745 miles.
- Glacier National Park has 762 lakes. The largest is Lake McDonald at 9.4 miles long and 1.5 miles wide. The park also has 563 streams, totaling 1,606 miles. The longest stream is McDonald Creek at 25.8 miles.
- The park has 429 archeological sites, including more than 50 vision quest sites.

WATERTON LAKES NATIONAL PARK FAST FACTS

- Unlike most U.S. national parks, Waterton has a year-round residential community. Waterton Townsite, with a summertime population of about 2,500, offers lodging, dining, supplies, and recreational services to locals and tourists. This quaint mountain village is the park's vibrant center.

🖋 Known as, "where the mountains meet the prairies," the Waterton area was protected as a forest preserve in 1895.

🖋 Waterton Lakes National Park encompasses 195 square miles.

🖋 There are more than 100 miles of maintained hiking trails in Waterton.

🖋 Waterton Lakes National Park ranges in elevation from 4,232 feet at the townsite to 9,547 at Mount Blakiston.

🖋 Waterton Lakes National Park was Canada's fourth national park.

🖋 There are more than 60 species of mammals, and 24 species of fish.

🖋 Waterton–Glacier became the first international park in the world in 1932. Both were designated UNESCO World Heritage Sites in 1995.

TEN THINGS YOU MAY NOT KNOW
ABOUT GLACIER & WATERTON

- There is no granite in Glacier National Park. Prospectors working claims in the 1890s thought the Purcell lava was granite.
- Glacier Park Lodge is not in the park.
- There are no venomous snakes in Glacier National Park.
- Although winter does not officially begin until December 21, that month has the second highest snowfall behind January.
- Drowning is the number one cause of fatalities in Glacier National Park.
- Grizzly bears are good swimmers, have no problem running downhill, and most can climb trees.
- Glacier National Park is open year-round. You can hike, bicycle, ski, and snowshoe when the roads are barricaded to automobiles.
- Going-to-the-Sun Road is not a highway. Long ago, it was decided that the Department of the Interior would maintain the road and not the Department of Transportation.
- James Willard Schultz's book, *Signposts of Adventure*, provided Blackfeet names to many of the features on the east side of the park.
- Waterton Lakes gained federal protection as a forest park 15 years before Glacier.

AN EXTREMELY BRIEF GEOLOGIC HISTORY OF GLACIER–WATERTON

Three big geologic events formed what would become Waterton–Glacier International Peace Park: rock formation, mountain building, and glacial carving.

About 1.5 billion years ago, a shallow sea covered the area 65 miles west of the park. Water runoff from surrounding hills deposited mud and sand. As animals with shells died, they left behind lime deposits. Layers of colored mud, sand, and lime collected over millions of years. The weight of new deposits compressed earlier strata toward the Earth's mantle. This pressure, along with heat from the mantle, changed the deposits into sedimentary rocks. The rock remained undisturbed for about a billion years.

Plate tectonics, the driving force of continental drift, began to act on the rock layers about 150 million years ago. The dry seabed was pushed eastward over the next 110 million years as a gigantic four-mile-thick slab of flat rock. The slab pushed up and over a wall of immovable rock. A mountain range was formed that looked different than today's landscape which was sculpted by a different event.

About two million years ago the Earth's climate cooled, and enormous sheets of ice spread over North America as far south as present-day Montana. A cap of ice covered the mountains to a depth of more than one mile. The ice responded to the force of gravity, grinding, scraping, and carving the rock layers as it moved. This event glaciated the region. The ice melted about 11,000 years ago, leaving the mountains, lakes, rivers, and valleys that you enjoy today. A lesser ice age is responsible for the alpine glaciers that remain.

A SHORT CULTURAL HISTORY OF THE GLACIER–WATERTON AREA

Photo by James W. Schultz, MSU-Bozeman Library, image 33, Collection 10.

People have roamed here for at least 13,000 years. The area was the exclusive home of Native Americans—the Blackfeet, Blood, Kalispel, and Kootenai people—before non-native fur trappers from the east began showing up 300 years ago.

By the 1850s, interest in trapping faded, but the mountain men had blazed trails into wilderness that allowed others, seeking different forms of wealth, to follow. Prospectors combed the mountains looking for gold and silver. Mining claims were established in the Swiftcurrent Valley, around Cracker Lake, Lake Josephine, and the Grinnell Valley. All of these areas were on the western portion of Blackfeet territory. The miners found little gold, and the diggings were abandoned by 1900.

Prospectors searching for precious metals discovered oil in the Kintla Lake area in what would become Glacier National Park and in the Cameron Creek drainage of today's Waterton Lakes National Park. Oil companies formed almost overnight, but the wells proved unprofitable, and drilling soon stopped.

The final attempt to make a fortune off the resources in today's Glacier National Park area was the logging of the old growth trees around Lake McDonald in 1906. Influential residents of Montana's Flathead Valley resisted this short-sighted venture. They rallied behind others supporting the creation of a national park and stopped the logging project.

Each park had its champions—people who conceived the idea of protecting the area's natural and cultural heritage for the enjoyment of future generations. Four people stand out as campaigners for the future parks: James Willard Schultz, George Grinnell, F.W. Godsal, and Kootenai Brown.

The first documented European to explore Canada's Waterton Lakes area was Lieutenant Thomas Blakiston in 1858. He named it after Charles Waterton, a prominent British naturalist. A local rancher, F.W. Godsal, lobbied for the Waterton area's protection as early as 1893. It was granted protected status as a Dominion Forest Park in 1895. John George Kootenai Brown, an early settler, served as the area's first game guardian and fisheries inspector, and in 1911 became Waterton Lakes National Park's first superintendent. Waterton Townsite was laid out by the time that Glacier National Park was officially protected.

James Willard Schultz was 17 in 1876 when he arrived in present-day Montana to work at a trading post. The Blackfeet people accepted him as one of their own and named him Apikuni, "Far-Off White Robe." Schultz lived closely with his new family, even going with them on raids against other tribes. He soon began to write about his experiences, sending stories to magazines like *Forest and Stream*. The magazine's editor, George Bird Grinnell, was inspired, and sought out Schultz as a guide to show him the region. Both Schultz and Grinnell, through their passionate writing about the future park, campaigned for Glacier's protection. Their efforts paid off when on May 11, 1910, President William H. Taft signed legislation that saved it forever.

The interests of many people came together to establish both parks as popular destinations, and no one was more influential than Louis W. Hill, president of the Great Northern Railway. Under the direction of Louis' father, James J. Hill, the railroad completed its transcontinental route over Marias Pass in 1891. Louis realized that the railroad could bring vacationers from the east to visit the Crown of the Continent. And that is exactly what happened. Tourists traveled to East Glacier or Belton on a Great Northern passenger train and, while touring, they stayed in hotels and chalets built by the railroad company, including the Prince of Wales Hotel, Many Glacier Hotel, Glacier Park Lodge, Sperry Chalet, and Granite Park Chalet. Lake McDonald Lodge was built by private entrepreneurs and later sold, in 1930, to the National Park Service.

The proximity of Waterton Lakes and Glacier National Parks helped spawn a new idea. The Rotary Clubs of Alberta and Montana conceived the concept of an international park. Waterton–Glacier International Peace Park was commemorated in 1932 as an expression that two countries could solve their differences without conflict. Since then, the Peace Park's example of cooperation in natural and cultural heritage management has inspired similar efforts in southern Africa, Korea, and the Middle East.

GEORGE BIRD GRINNELL

Photo by T. J. Hileman, 1925, National Park Service.

George Bird Grinnell was a renowned natural history expert. His fame led to an invitation to serve as a naturalist on George Armstrong Custer's expedition to the Black Hills in 1874. Custer was so impressed with Grinnell's work that he asked him to accompany the Seventh Cavalry on its tour of duty of the Little Bighorn in 1876. Grinnell declined because of work responsibilities at Yale University. It was fortunate for Grinnell because he might have been killed, along with Custer, at the Battle of the Little Bighorn. If so, today's Glacier National Park would have lost a strong supporter who would be instrumental in promoting it as a national park.

For 35 years, Grinnell was the editor of Forest and Stream, the leading natural history magazine of its day. He also helped found the Audubon Society, the Boone and Crockett Club, and the New York Zoological Society. Grinnell also served as an advisor to President Theodore Roosevelt. After many years exploring the mountains and glaciers of what he called the "Crown of the Continent," he worked tirelessly for the protection of Glacier as a national park. Some people have referred to Grinnell as the Father of Glacier National Park. He died in 1938 at the age of 89.

BEST SCENIC DRIVES

What is the best way to see Glacier National Park? It depends. It depends on the time of year, how adventurous you are, and how much time you have to spend in the park. During the summer, there are several ways to experience Glacier. You may choose to bicycle, hike, or see it by motor vehicle. The best ways to see the park by vehicle are the free shuttle service, the Red Buses, or your own car. This section describes the best scenic drives in Waterton–Glacier International Peace Park.

1. Going-to-the-Sun Road

If you have only one day to see Glacier National Park, then travel the Going-to-the-Sun Road. Though you will not be alone, the stunning scenery is well worth the drive. The National Park Service estimates that 90 percent of the 2 million annual visitors stay only one day, and most of their time is spent viewing from the car.

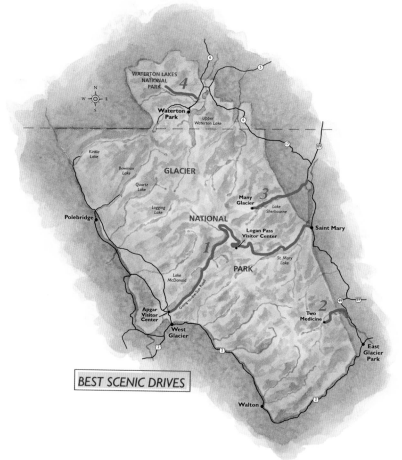

BEST SCENIC DRIVES

Going-to-the-Sun Road has scenic vistas, interpretive waysides, trailheads to lure you, visitor centers, and concessions. You will begin to appreciate why the Blackfeet people referred to this land as the "Shining Mountains" and the "Backbone of the World."

Tour promoters have called it "The American Alps," and early conservationist George Bird Grinnell called Glacier National Park the "Crown of the Continent," referring to the fact that it straddles the Continental Divide.

The following are must-see stops along Going-to-the-Sun Road from the western entrance to St. Mary.

Apgar Village

The village is home to Apgar Visitor Center, shops, a cafe, and lodging. Park and walk to the shore of Lake McDonald. Going-to-the-Sun Road hugs the east shore of the lake and then climbs into the mountains beyond.

Lake McDonald Lodge

Park in the large lot and go into the lodge. You entered through one of the two back doors. Originally, these were designated for lodge employees and trail riders. The Going-to-the-Sun Road reached the lodge in 1922, eight years after the lodge was completed in 1914. The front of the lodge faces Lake McDonald, where early-day guests arrived by boat from Apgar. Modeled after a Swiss hunting lodge, it attracted several luminary personalities soon after opening, including U.S. senators, Will Rogers, and Charlie Russell. Walk across the lobby and through the front door. Generations of visitors have enjoyed this serene view of the lake.

The Lodge Camp Store is a good place to purchase snacks and picnic items. Or grab a bite at one of two restaurants here. The next available food is at Rising Sun, 11.8 miles east of Logan Pass.

Sacred Dancing Cascade

A short trail and footbridge get you close to the sight, sound, and feel of this lyrically named series of small waterfalls. The name is a translation from the Kootenai Indian language meaning a good place to dance. Long ago, a band of the Kootenai performed their ceremonial Blacktail Deer Dance in this area.

Trail of the Cedars Nature Trail

This short, easy walk begins just north of Avalanche Campground. The boardwalk and paved trail with interpretive signs loop through a grove of mature western redcedar and western hemlock trees to a beautiful gorge. This is one of the most popular trails in the park. Parking is limited.

The Loop

Almost a mile north of the West Tunnel, Going-to-the-Sun Road makes a 180-degree hairpin turn at "The Loop." A small parking area and restrooms are located here. The Loop provides excellent views of the Livingston Range, and the headwaters area of the McDonald Creek Valley. Stop for the view and read the interpretive signs about the effects of forest fires across the valley on Heavens Peak.

Bird Woman Falls Overlook

This small pullout offers dramatic views toward Logan Pass and across the valley to 492-foot Bird Woman Falls cascading from the bowl below Mount Oberlin and Clements Mountain.

The Weeping Wall

To this point along the road, you have seen water flowing in creeks, water falling over rock faces, and water tumbling down the sides of the cut road. None of these compare to the wonder that awaits you at the Weeping Wall. What causes the wall to weep? A combination of surface run-off and underground springs exposed during the construction of Going-to-the-Sun Road created this exciting feature. Remember to roll up your windows. The water's cold!

Big Bend

Park here for views of McDonald Creek Valley and the Weeping Wall. You will likely be entertained by one of the largest members of the squirrel family: the yellow-bellied marmot. If you were a marmot, you would spend summer days feeding on grasses and staying vigilant for predators like eagles, badgers, grizzly bears, wolves, and mountain lions. Look for the big furry rodent among the rocks and listen for its warning whistle.

Oberlin Bend

This pullout is at a tight turn 0.3 mile west of Logan Pass. A short trail leads you to a viewing platform. Mid-morning to late afternoon offers the best lighting for appreciating the depth of the vista. To your right is Pollock Mountain, the Garden Wall through which the Highline Trail passes, Bishops Cap, and Haystack Butte. The Logan Creek drainage stretches out below you. The line of mountains in the distance is the Livingston Range. To your immediate left is Oberlin Mountain.

Logan Pass

You've made it to the top! Grab your camera. Take a deep breath of the exhilarating alpine air. Walk past the visitor center and up the path leading to the Hidden Lake overlook. You don't need to go all the way to the overlook to get a sense of Logan Pass' timeless beauty. From the trail, the tableau is stunning in every direction. At your feet, a floral carpet progresses through the short summer, first dominated by glades of glacier lilies, then alpine asters. Look for Columbian ground squirrels feeding on the grasses, bighorn sheep lolling in small groups, and bright, white-haired mountain goats scampering among steep slopes. The goats you chance upon near the Hidden Lake overlook are nonchalant, apparently willing to pose before breathtaking backdrops. You'll show your friends a picture worthy of *National Geographic*.

Logan Pass crosses the Continental Divide. Water that drains on the east side of the Divide flows toward the Atlantic Ocean while precipitation on the west side drains to the Pacific Ocean. Make sure that you explore the visitor center before you leave. It is full of interpretive displays about life at Logan Pass.

Find a vacant bench on a trail just west of the visitor center. Here you can sit and take in the peacefulness of this high alpine environment.

East Side Tunnel Area

There are five turnouts along this part of the Going-to-the-Sun Road.

The pullouts afford you exciting panoramic views of the U-shaped, glaciated St. Mary Creek drainage, and of Logan Pass. Picture yourself standing on the mile-high glacier that was here 20,000 years ago while wondering what the valley below would look like someday. Today is that day.

Jackson Glacier Overlook

This pullout is a mile southeast of Siyeh Bend. This is the only overlook from which it is obvious that you are seeing a glacier. An interpretive sign points the way. Why is the glacier blue? Jackson Glacier is compressed ice. It appears blue because dense ice reflects the blue light present in sunlight.

Sunrift Gorge

Treat yourself to a geologic wonder. It is only 200 feet from the road along a paved path. A weakness in the rock has allowed the creek to erode a fissure into a narrow, winding, and beautiful chasm. Observe plant growth along the sheer walls. Look for birds navigating the crevasse, as you feel the moist bracing air.

Sun Point ➤

Take a short walk from the picnic area to Sun Point. A direction finder identifies many of the peaks that scrape the sky south of St. Mary Lake.

Wild Goose Island

Looking for an unforgettable photo showing that you visited Glacier National Park? Snap one of Wild Goose Island in St. Mary Lake, and you will have one of the most iconic images in the United States. Linger and reflect on the serenity of the grand landscape.

Rising Sun

You will pass through several aspen groves from here to the park entrance. Gnarled tree trunks show the effects of lashing winds that sometimes pummel the park's east side.

◄ Triple Divide Peak Turnout

There is only one place in the United States where water can flow to the Atlantic Ocean, the Pacific Ocean, or to Hudson Bay. An interpretive sign here helps you locate 8,020-foot Triple Divide Peak, across St. Mary Lake to the south.

St. Mary River Bridge ▾

The St. Mary River begins near Jackson Glacier, flows through St. Mary Lake, and continues its flow here. Where is this water going? It flows to the northeast and empties into Canada's Hudson Bay.

▾ St. Mary Visitor Center

Here, exhibits link the region's history with the world views of the Indian tribes who consider the Glacier National Park area their homeland. Upon leaving the park, you enter the Blackfeet Reservation. When you

return home, you can once again enjoy this area's panoramic view, follow the weather, and see the changing sunlight by visiting Glacier's web page, and clicking on the webcams page.

If you have more than one day to tour the park, I recommend two additional scenic drives that are both on the park's east side: Two Medicine Valley and Many Glacier. A third option is to drive the Red Rock Parkway in Waterton Lakes National Park.

2. Two Medicine Valley

Somewhat off the beaten path, Two Medicine Valley is typically less crowded and affords great opportunities to hike, camp, picnic, boat, photograph, or simply bask in the scenery. From MT 49, Two Medicine Road skirts the north shore of Lower Two Medicine Lake. After 4 miles you'll reach the entrance station. Continue west 1 mile to the trailhead for Running Eagle Falls (see page 56). Another

4 miles brings you to Two Medicine Lake, bounded on the north by Rising Wolf Mountain, with the craggy pyramid of Sinopah Mountain jutting up from the head of the lake. Facilities here include a 99-site campground, camp store (the only remaining building of the old Two Medicine Chalet compound; see page 66), a picnic area, and boat tours. Trails circle the main lake and branch off to three passes on the Continental Divide.

The turnoff to the Two Medicine Valley is on MT 49, 4 miles north of the town of East Glacier Park or 26 miles south of St. Mary on US 89 and MT 49.

3. Many Glacier Road

Glacier National Park is known as a "hiker's park," and Many Glacier boasts the greatest concentration of trailheads in the park, each leading to a sparkling lake, glacier, high pass, or peak. This bonanza of trails, combined with spectacular scenery and ample wildlife, makes Many Glacier the most popular destination on the park's east side.

From St. Mary, drive 8.6 miles north on US 89 to Babb and turn left on Many Glacier Road (Route 3), which follows Swiftcurrent

Creek west. In just under 5 miles, the road leaves the Blackfeet Reservation and enters the park near the foot of 6-mile-long Lake Sherburne. The open valley offers good views of mountains to the west. The Many Glacier entrance station is 7.4 miles from Babb. At mile 10.4, a trailhead on the right provides access to a 1-mile hike to Apikuni Falls.

At the 12-mile mark, a left turn leads across Swiftcurrent Creek to the historic Many Glacier Hotel, the largest of the park's lodges. Park in the upper lot to tour the hotel or stroll the shores of Swiftcurrent Lake. Trails here lead to Cracker Lake, Piegan Pass, and Grinnell Glacier. Return to the main road and go left to reach Many Glacier Campground, the Swiftcurrent Motor Inn and Cabins, and a store and restaurant at road's end. Watch for bighorn sheep, mountain goats, and bears on the flanks of Mount Henkel and Altyn Peak to the north. Trails here lead to Grinnell Glacier, Swiftcurrent Pass, and Iceberg and Ptarmigan lakes.

4. Red Rock Parkway – Waterton

Waterton Lakes National Park is known as *where the mountains meet the prairies.* You can get a sense of what this means by traveling the Red Rock Parkway and reading the interpretive messages posted at the turnouts. The parkway takes you from rolling prairie, along Blakiston Creek, and into a canyon walled in by lofty peaks. You are rewarded at the end of the road with access to Red Rock Canyon, and a nature walk to stretch

your legs while learning about the area's geology. This is the best drive in Waterton for chancing upon wildlife.

Best "Leave-the-Driving-to-Us" Options

You have options if you are tired of driving after a long trip to the park, or don't want to navigate the mountain roads. A free shuttle service runs the length of Going-to-the-Sun Road from early July to Labor Day. Also, several companies operate excursions within the park. They travel Going-to-the-Sun Road and other areas as well. One is a historical symbol harkening back to the early days of motor touring in Glacier National Park: The Red Buses.

Glacier's Red Bus Service

You can still enjoy 1930s high-life touring by traveling in one of the classic Red Buses that originally went into service in 1936. By 1939, a fleet  of 33 Mountain Ash Berry Red buses, made by the White Motor Company, provided an unequalled roadway experience. As drivers could be heard jamming the manual transmissions into gear crossing the Continental Divide, they gained the nickname "Jammers." Don't be concerned about traveling in an old bus; the entire fleet was updated to modern standards in 2002. The open-air coaches assure you multi-sensory wonders—the sights, sounds, and fragrances of the park, along with plenty of alpine sunshine.

Several tour itineraries are available. Reservations are required; see the phone number in the Resources section at the back of this book.

Glacier National Park's Free Shuttle System

Want to tour Going-to-the-Sun Road for free and yet have the freedom to investigate along the way? The free Glacier shuttle service offers stops at all the "must see" locations along Going-to-the-Sun Road. Hop on at St. Mary or Apgar, and hop off at any stop that piques your interest. Discover, hike, photograph, and then board another shuttle to your next destination, and share your experiences with fellow riders.

David Restivo, National Park Service.

A little planning will help you get the most out of the shuttle system. Refer to the *Waterton–Glacier Guide* newspaper (available at entrance stations and visitor centers) for up-to-date information about times and stops. Also, be prepared with plenty of water, snacks, proper clothing, bear spray, and a day pack to carry your items. The Glacier shuttle service is the best way to share your excitement of the park with other people.

BEST ROADSIDE PICNIC AREAS

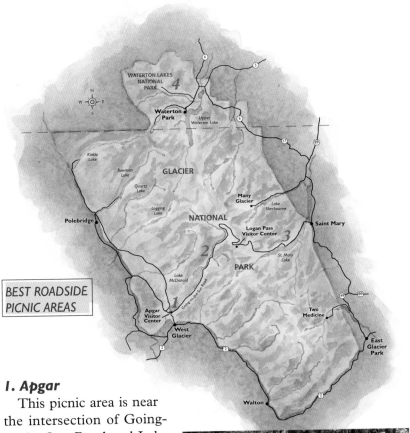

BEST ROADSIDE
PICNIC AREAS

I. Apgar

This picnic area is near the intersection of Going-to-the-Sun Road and Lake View Drive. Most of the sites are dotted under a grove of pines near the Lake McDonald shoreline. A few steps through the wooded area from your picnic table give you commanding views of the lake. The afternoon

Gabriel Morrow, National Park Service.

light reflects off the mountains to the northeast, making this an exceptional choice for a summer stop.

2. Avalanche Creek

A favorite of locals, this large picnic area borders the confluence of Avalanche Creek and McDonald Creek. It is a very busy area, yet some of the sites have a secluded feel. Beautiful McDonald Creek is a great place to cool your feet and search for wildflowers and aquatic insects along the shoreline.

3. Rising Sun

Tucked in a cottonwood grove along the shore of St. Mary Lake, this picnic area offers great views of Otokomi Mountain to the north and Red Eagle Mountain across the lake. Children can run and play on the open fields here, and the Rising Sun Store across the road offers provisions to make your picnic complete. Bears frequent this area all summer, so don't leave food or coolers unattended and make sure that your site is spotless before you leave.

4. Lost Horse Creek – Waterton

The Lost Horse Creek Picnic Area is adjacent to the Red Rock Parkway, 5 miles northwest of Crandell Mountain Campground. Children can explore the shallow and colorful creek while you prepare a meal in the picnic shelter. This site accommodates one or two groups, making it a "Best," if you want privacy. Stay alert, you are in the center of bear country. Black bears rove the meadow across the parkway.

National Park Service.

BEST NATURE TRAILS

A walk is the best way to get a complete sensory experience in Glacier National Park. Hiking opportunities abound. Not up for a long backpack or a strenuous climb? Good news! Each area of the park has at least one short, gentle trail. Most of these are interpretive, with brochures and signage provided by the National Park Service and the Glacier Natural History Association. Tired of being in your car? Pull over and walk these trails!

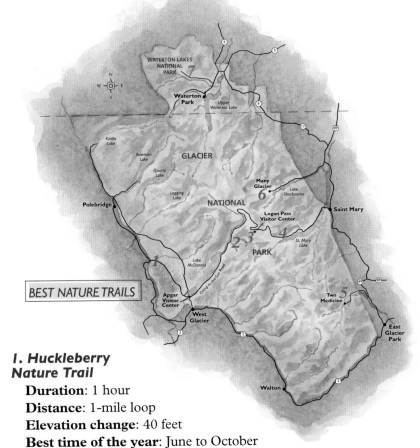

1. Huckleberry Nature Trail

Duration: 1 hour

Distance: 1-mile loop

Elevation change: 40 feet

Best time of the year: June to October

Trailhead: The trailhead is just inside the park's eastern boundary, on the Camas Creek Road about 11 miles north of Apgar Village. The official park visitor map shows this as the Forest and Fire Trail. Interpretive pamphlets are available at Apgar Visitor Center.

Walking directions: This trail begins at the south end of the parking lot. Walk about 0.1 mile to reach the loop. Continue to your left.

Special attention: Experience forest succession. This area of Huckleberry Mountain burns on a recurring basis. Until 2001, this forest was made up of lodgepole pine and western larch. Between August and October of that year, the Moose Fire consumed most of the vegetation, including the lodgepole pine and western larch. Lodgepole pines, however, are uniquely adapted to fire. Their cones are resinous, sealed and protected in pitch until the extreme heat of a forest fire melts the pitch. The cones then open and release their

seeds. Lodgepole are among the first seeds to germinate after a fire, giving them a growing advantage over other tree species. Most of the young trees you see here started growing soon after the Moose Fire. It may be a long time before another fire sweeps this area. If you return every few years to the Huckleberry Nature Trail, you will see how the forest matures through the succession process.

2. Trail of the Cedars

Duration: 30 minutes to one hour

Distance: 1-mile loop

Elevation change: 10 feet

Best time of the year: June to October

Trailhead: The trail starts just north of the Avalanche Creek bridge on Going-to-the-Sun Road.

Walking directions: Begin your hike on the boardwalk immediately north of the Avalanche Creek bridge.

Special attention: Parking is limited. Visitors use this area for picnicking at McDonald Creek picnic grounds, hiking to Avalanche

Lake, and walking the Trail of the Cedars. When the park is busy, plan to arrive before 10 a.m. or after 4 p.m.

This is the most popular loop trail in Glacier National Park. The loop is short, easy to walk, and has beautiful, diverse scenery. The Glacier Natural History Association and the National Park Service have installed signs along the boardwalk to interpret the natural history of this cottonwood-western redcedar riparian forest.

Linger on this trail, and give yourself the opportunity to take in the sounds, fragrances, temperature variations, and sights of this unique grove. This part of the park has not burned in many decades, due in part to the damp microclimate. Some of the western redcedars you are walking among started growing in 1653, when New York City was first incorporated and still a Dutch possession.

The first half of the trail is on a boardwalk. The trail becomes a footpath after crossing a bridge over Avalanche Creek. The upstream canyon is one of the most photographed locations in the park. The trail to Avalanche Lake is on the west side of the bridge. A good side trip is to walk this trail for a few hundred yards. Here the creek has cut a narrow canyon into red argillite rock. The swirling waters, turquoise pools, and sculpted red rock draw onlookers and photographers. Stay back from the edge; the footing can be slippery.

The remaining Trail of the Cedars is a paved footpath with several benches for you to sit and enjoy the creek and the area's splendor. This section is in an abandoned loop of the Avalanche Creek Campground. The campground was one of the facilities improved by the Civilian Conservation Corps (CCC) in the 1930s. The trail ends at Going-to-the-Sun Road just south of the bridge over Avalanche Creek.

3. Hidden Lake Overlook

Duration: 1 to 2 hours

Distance: 3 miles round-trip

Elevation change: 550 feet

Best time of the year: July to October

Trailhead: The trailhead is behind the Logan Pass Visitor Center. Parking is often limited July to September between 10 a.m. and 3 p.m. You can avoid the gamble of finding a parking space by using the free Glacier Shuttle System from either Apgar or St. Mary.

Walking directions: The trail begins as a paved path, changes to a boardwalk, and then becomes a pathway over broken rock.

Special attention: The Glacier Natural History Association and the National Park Service have provided a trail guide for the Hidden Lake

Trail, available at the trailhead.

An estimated 3,000 people visit Logan Pass on any given day in July and August. The trail to the Hidden Lake Overlook is the most popular walk in Glacier National Park. Many visitors do not make the entire trip to the overlook. A large number will walk at least a portion of the Hidden Lake Trail, content to take photographs of the landscape, wildflowers, animals, or family portraits with a spectacular backdrop.

On the lower reaches of the trail you will see myriad wildflowers that bloom during the park's short growing season. The diversity and color of the wildflower display is stunning during July, August, and early September. The short growing season means that few of these plants are annuals, needing to progress through the life cycle of seed germination to flowering, seed development, and dispersal in a single season. Instead, the plants at this altitude are perennials: flowering from well-established roots and bulbs.

Some of the plants flowering around you are a century old. Others, like the glacier lily, are short-lived perennials that begin growing before "winter" ends. They push up through the snow and flower as the snow melts around them. Many species are fragile and have only a few days to bloom, be pollinated, and begin seed development.

Look for mountain goats, bighorn sheep, marmots, and pikas toward the upper part of the trail.

You reach Hidden Lake Overlook at 1.5 miles. The observation platform allows you a panoramic view of the mountains near Logan Pass: Oberlin, Bear Hat, and Reynolds. Below, Hidden Lake is a mirror on calm days, a glimmer of alternating colors on windy days. The trail continues 1.5 miles down to Hidden Lake (with a strenuous return climb), or turn around here and head back to Logan Pass.

4. Baring Falls

Duration: 1 hour

Distance: 1.4 miles round-trip

Elevation change: 40 feet

Best time of the year: June to October

Trailhead: The trailhead is at the southeast corner of the Sun Point parking lot off Going-to-the-Sun Road above St. Mary Lake.

Walking directions: The trail to Baring Falls follows the Sun Point Nature Trail and is a gentle pathway along the north shore of St. Mary Lake.

Special attention: The Glacier Natural History Association and the National Park Service have provided a trail guide for the Sun Point Nature Trail, available at the trailhead.

The rocky, heavily used, and well-maintained trail descends toward St. Mary Lake. The trail soon splits: the main trail goes to your right and a spur trail forks to the left, leading to Sun Point and views of St. Mary Lake. At 9.6 miles long, 0.25 mile wide, and 289 feet deep, St. Mary Lake is the second largest in the park. Glaciers "bulldozed" this area 10,000 years ago, leaving hanging valleys and this lake as proof of their ability to shape the landscape. An interpretive panel at Sun Point identifies the mountains in view.

Return to the trail junction and follow the main trail west. You are now in the area of the Going-to-the-Sun Chalets that were constructed 100 feet above the lake. Built by the Great Northern Railway in 1913, the chalet complex included nine buildings with a main lodge, an employee dormitory, and guest quarters. Only photographs remain of the chalet buildings. Poor maintenance resulted in disrepair. Visitors sought other accommodations, so the buildings were razed in 1949.

You will soon see a footbridge that crosses Baring Creek. To the right is Baring Falls, at one time named Water Ouzel Falls for its resident American dipper birds *(Cinclus mexicanus)*. Look for slate-gray dippers flying, wading, and bobbing near the waterfall as they search for aquatic insects and small fish. From here, the trail continues west to St. Mary Falls (see page 30). Or turn around to return to Sun Point.

5. Running Eagle Falls

Duration: 30 minutes to 1 hour
Distance: 0.3 mile round-trip
Elevation change: None
Best time of the year: July to September
Trailhead: The Running Eagle Falls Trailhead is 1 mile west of the Two Medicine entrance station on Two Medicine Road, off MT Highway 49. There is ample parking.
Walking directions: There are two possible paths to follow. One begins near the bridge and is wide, gentle, and not paved. The other path begins from the center of the parking lot and is paved. The trails converge before arriving at the confluence of Dry Creek and Two Medicine Creek.

Special attention: The Glacier Natural History Association and the National Park Service have provided a Running Eagle Falls nature trail guide, available at the parking lot trailhead. The short walk to Running Eagle Falls is a refreshing stroll through a lush riparian forest. The trail guide relates the story of Running Eagle (Pitamakan), a woman warrior, in English and in the Blackfeet language. The guide also provides background on the Blackfeet People's traditional and medicinal uses for some of the plants you will encounter along the trail.

Running Eagle Falls is close to the trailhead, making it accessible to almost any walker. Because of its geology, this unique waterfall changes depending on the water volume in Two Medicine Creek. High water obscures the water issuing from the cave outlet. In late summer, stream flow may be too low to breach the precipice, and water flows only out of the cave below. Between high and low water flow, it is possible to see water emerging from the cave and over the top. This is a great waterfall to photograph any time of the year—morning is best.

6. Swiftcurrent Nature Trail

Duration: 2 to 3 hours

Distance: 2.6-mile loop

Elevation change: 10 feet

Best time of the year: June to October

Trailhead: There are two access points to the Swiftcurrent Nature Trail. One trailhead is at the parking lot of the picnic area at the Grinnell Lake Trail Trailhead, 0.5 mile west of the turnoff to Many Glacier Hotel on Many Glacier Road. The second access is near the shoreline of Swiftcurrent Lake at the south end of Many Glacier Hotel. To start from the latter trailhead, park in the upper lot above the hotel.

Walking directions: You can begin your walk at either trailhead. Halfway around Swiftcurrent Lake you will encounter a junction with the Grinnell Glacier Trail. Walk 0.2 mile along this trail to see picturesque Lake Josephine. This short trail is paved. Look to your right from the Lake Josephine boat dock, and search for the rock tailings of the Josephine Mine, an old copper mine.

Special attention: This entire trail travels through bear and moose country. Even on bright summer days, with many visitors using the trail, you could be surprised by a bear or moose walking out of the deep understory and onto the trail. Use your "visiting bear country" skills (see page 83).

This is a self-guided nature trail. National Park Service pamphlets are available at both trailheads. The pamphlets do not specify stops along the trail but provide information about the natural history of the Swiftcurrent Lake area.

The forest here is home to subalpine fir, lodgepole pine, spruce, and aspen. The understory includes snowberry (look for white berries in August), serviceberry (sometimes confused with huckleberries), thimbleberry (grizzly and black bears eat them), as well as several fern species and myriad mushroom types. To complete the loop, cross the road bridge over the outlet of Swiftcurrent Lake and follow the road back to your car.

7. Red Rock Canyon – Waterton

Duration: 30 minutes
Distance: 0.4-mile loop
Difficulty: Easy
Elevation change: 30 feet
Best time of the year: Spring through autumn
Trailhead: Follow the Red Rock Parkway from its junction with Canada Highway 5 west about 9 miles to Red Rock Canyon parking area.

Walking directions: Go across the footbridge at the south end of the parking lot. Turn north and follow the trail along the canyon. The trail crosses the canyon in 0.2 mile and returns to the parking lot.

Special attention: Signs along the trail interpret the natural history of Red Rock Canyon. You'll discover the age of the canyon and why the rocks are red. The lower reaches of the canyon offer pools and swift water coursing over smooth chutes worn in the rock. This is a favorite location for water play on a July afternoon.

BEST DAY HIKES

I. Avalanche Lake

Level of difficulty: Easy
Duration: 2 to 3 hours
Distance: 4.2 miles round-trip
Elevation change: 500 feet
Best time of the year: June through October

Trailhead: The trail starts just north of Avalanche Creek Campground on Going-to-the-Sun Road.

Hiking directions: South of the Avalanche Creek Bridge, you will find a sign for Avalanche Lake. Follow the paved path for 0.1 mile to a second sign just before the bridge over

Avalanche Creek; turn right for the trail to Avalanche Lake.

Special note: Avalanche Lake is an excellent example of a cirque lake. Parking is limited between 10 a.m. and 4 p.m. on busy days. Plan to arrive early, or use the free shuttle service.

The hike: The hike begins in an abandoned loop of the Avalanche Creek Campground. Watch for the turn-off to Avalanche Lake at 0.1 mile. Before turning right and climbing the short rise, walk another 100 feet to the bridge over Avalanche Creek at the mouth of a photogenic gorge.

Go back to the turn-off and continue your hike to the lake. The next 0.3 mile parallels Avalanche Creek Canyon. Smooth-sculpted red argillite rock chutes connect swirling turquoise pools. The features entice you to draw near; be careful, the rocks are slippery.

About 1 mile in, a large blow-down along Hidden Creek allows views of the sheer south faces of Mount Cannon, where mountains goats often rest on small ledges. At 1.5 miles the trail begins to climb. From here to the foot of the lake you will hike through a sparse forest of hemlock, larch, redcedar, red maple, and black cottonwood. The trail is often covered with lush mosses, providing soft footing. You will pass through dense undergrowth of thimbleberry, elderberry, and bracken ferns as you approach the lake.

At an elevation of 3,905 feet, Avalanche Lake pools in a depression left by a melting glacier. Today, the lake's water comes from the Sperry Glacier basin and the surrounding mountains. Facing the lake you can identify, from left to right, Bear Hat Mountain (8,684 feet), Fusillade Mountain (8,750 feet), Little Matterhorn (7,886 feet), and Mount Brown (8,565 feet). Five cascades feed the lake. Monument Falls sprays between Bear Hat and Fusillade mountains. Out of sight, Sperry Glacier rests in the hanging cirque valley between Fusillade and Little Matterhorn.

A trail continues on the west side to the head of the lake with access to the main inlet stream and gravel beaches. You may be drawn to explore the high country beyond Avalanche Lake, but dense brush, cliffs, and poor footing make off-trail travel inadvisable for even the most experienced hikers. Better to bring binoculars and scan the slopes for wildlife from the comfort of a sunny spot on the lakeshore.

2. The Garden Wall

Level of difficulty: Easy to moderate

Duration: 4 to 5 hours

Distance: 7 miles round-trip

Elevation change: 400 feet

Best time of the year: July through October

Trailhead: North of the Logan Pass Visitor Center parking lot across Going-to-the-Sun Road.

Hiking directions: Follow the Highline Trail. This hike begins at the sign at Logan Pass signifying the Highline Trail. Walk 3.5 miles to the Haystack Butte saddle and then retrace your steps to Logan Pass.

Special note: One July afternoon, I encountered what looked like a bear cub loping toward me on the trail. I froze. Was a sow near? The creature detected me. Alarmed, it skittered downhill. Its profile and long furry tail told me that I had seen my first wolverine. Wildlife abounds along this busy trail.

The hike: Begin your hike in the early morning to enjoy the soft light reflecting off Reynolds Mountain, Heavens Peak, the Livingston Range, and Haystack Butte. The first 0.25 mile runs downhill, passing through an alpine meadow. Mountain goat ewes and kids are common here. The next 100 yards of trail follows a narrow ledge high above Going-to-the-Sun Road. A chain attached to the cliff face provides a handgrip. The remainder of the trail to Haystack Butte is flat until the 3-mile mark. The last 0.5 mile is a long switchback terminating at the Haystack Butte saddle. When you arrive, you are between Haystack Mountain to the west and Mount Gould to the east. The mountain in front of you is Mount Grinnell. The saddle area is a good place for lunch. Golden-mantled ground squirrels will greet you, but please don't share your food.

Most of the trail parallels the Garden Wall, which forms the west face of the Continental Divide along 9,190-foot Pollock Mountain and 9,553-foot Mount Gould. The Garden Wall supports abundant wildlife, including mountain goats, marmots, pikas, chipmunks, Columbian ground squirrels, bears, and wolverines. Myriad springs and countless streamlets bathe the Garden Wall, making the trail intermittently muddy. The water nourishes a floral cornucopia. The beauty of the area is almost impossible to exaggerate. Throughout the summer season and well into autumn, the wildflower display can leave you in awe. Due to the short growing season, almost all of the plants are perennials. Some are much older than you are—many individual plants here are over 100 years old.

The Garden Wall faces west, receiving direct afternoon sunlight. It also receives the brunt of most weather systems. We think of alpine weather as severe, and yet the plants and animals along the Garden Wall are well adapted to this life zone and thrive here. Your tranquil backyard would be unlivable to them.

3. St. Mary Falls and Virginia Falls
Level of difficulty: Easy
Duration: 2 to 3 hours
Distance: 3.6 miles round-trip
Elevation change: 180 feet
Best time of the year: June through October
Trailhead: The trailhead is 10.5 miles west of St. Mary on Going-to-the-Sun Road, marked with a sign.
Hiking directions: The trail is well marked.
Special note: When the park is busy, you must arrive early in the morning or late in the afternoon to find parking.

The hike: Two hundred feet beyond the trailhead is a small south-facing meadow. This section of the trail is over red argillite, which is mudstone that is red because it was exposed to oxygen, coloring the iron-rich mud. Look for ripple marks on the large rock slabs along the trail.

National Park Service.

You are looking at a moment from 1.5 billion years ago preserved in stone. These ripple marks are the result of wave action over mud near the shore of the Belt Sea. The mud was buried under other deposits. The sea receded, and over time all of the deposits became sedimentary rock layers. This happened in present-day Washington. Beginning 60 million years ago, the rocks were pushed eastward and became part of the Rocky Mountains.

Follow the trail another 2 miles through a sun-flecked forest of Douglas-fir and maple trees, with an understory of beargrass, snowberry, and thimbleberry bushes. A bridge crosses over the St. Mary River just downstream from St. Mary Falls. Look for dippers (see page 90) around the base of the waterfall. The bridge is near the confluence of St. Mary River and Virginia Creek. Follow the trail along Virginia Creek another 0.6 mile to Virginia Falls. You will see that the creek is a series of cataracts and pools. The trail proceeds up a series of rocks steps and over a small bridge, which gives a good view of the waterfall. Use caution! The bridge and rocks are often slippery due to spray. The trail continues east above St. Mary Lake, but turn around here to return to the trailhead.

4. Scenic Point

Level of difficulty: Moderate
Duration: 4 to 5 hours
Distance: 6.5 miles round-trip
Elevation change: 2,358 feet
Best time of the year: July through October
Trailhead: The trailhead is 11.5 miles along Two Medicine Road from MT Highway 49.

Hiking directions: The trail sign reads "Mount Henry Trail."

Special attention: Scenic Point is the best destination to explore alpine tundra. Begin your hike in the morning to avoid climbing in the intense afternoon sun on the southwest-facing trail.

The hike: The trail begins as a narrow, somewhat flat track winding through a

Photo by Doug Bardwell.

subalpine fir, spruce, and pine forest. The understory includes beargrass and several grass species. Ruffed grouse, nuthatches, chickadees, and Clark's nutcrackers frequent the area. You encounter the Appistoki Falls Trail at 0.6 mile. The Appistoki Falls overlook is 200 feet up this spur. The experience is worth the diversion.

The Mount Henry Trail begins to climb and switchback on the east side of the Appistoki Creek drainage. You pass through several subalpine fir groves and patches of western white pines and follow a ridge above timberline at 2 miles. The trail climbs through a saddle and wraps around to the north, then east. You are now traversing through a fellfield, a term for tundra composed of 35 to 50 percent rock. Fellfields are shaped by wind and scant rocky soils. Here there are no large plants. Note the low-growing woody shrubs, mosses, lichens, and compact perennial flowers in plump round pillow shapes. Known as cushion plants, these perennials are adapted to the year-round cold, dry winds, intense sunlight, and nutrient-deficient soil. Avoid stepping on cushion plants; some are more than a century old and will crush under foot traffic.

Near the 3-mile mark, you will see a distant signpost ahead. The sign marks Scenic Point. Look for ripple marks and mud cracks in the red argillite rocks. These were formed in the Belt Sea, in present-day Washington, 1.5 billion years ago.

Scenic Point offers the easiest and best access to a 360-degree view. The vast Montana prairie is east. Below and to the south is East Glacier. The Great Bear Wilderness is distant to the southeast. The closest mountains south are Bison Mountain (7,834 feet), Medicine Peak (8,445 feet), Mount Henry (8,847 feet), and Appistoki Peak (8,164 feet). Looking west toward Two Medicine Lake, you see Sinopah Mountain (8,271 feet) and Mount Helen (8,538 feet). Rising Wolf Mountain (9,513 feet) dominates your northern view across the valley. Retrace your steps to return to the trailhead.

5. Iceberg Lake

Level of difficulty: Moderate
Duration: 5 to 6 hours
Distance: 9.5 miles round-trip
Elevation change: 1,194 feet
Best time of the year: July to early October
Trailhead: The Iceberg–Ptarmigan Trail starts from a small parking lot northwest of (and behind) the westernmost Swiftcurrent cabins at the end of Many Glacier Road. If that parking lot is full, park in the main lot in front of Swiftcurrent Motor Inn and walk back to the trailhead. Alternatively, you can start from the Swiftcurrent Pass Trailhead at the west end of the main lot and follow the signs for the Iceberg–Ptarmigan Trail.

Hiking directions: The web of both casual and official trails running through the undergrowth here can be confusing. The easiest way to find the trailhead is to walk up the asphalt driveway immediately west of Swiftcurrent Motor Inn. Stay on this road as it winds west and north about 500 feet to the small parking lot and signed trailhead. The trail goes right, into the trees, and begins climbing.

National Park Service.

Special note: You share this country with bears. The trail is often closed to allow grizzly bears to roam and feed undisturbed. While returning from Iceberg one August day, I encountered a grizzly sow and three cubs on the trail. She was feeding on huckleberries and showed no signs of leaving. The entertaining cubs made my 90-minute delay seem short. The trail was then closed for two days.

The hike: The trail contours along the western flank of 8,770-foot Mount Henkel and proceeds through groves of aspen and lodgepole pine, interspersed with meadows. Paintbrush, glacier lilies, asters, fireweed, beargrass, and roses flourish in the open spaces. The understory includes serviceberry, buffaloberry, snowberry, and huckleberry bushes. Mount Wilbur (9,321 feet) and Wilbur Creek are to the west as you climb 700 feet in the next 2.5 miles. At this point, you arrive at a bridge across Ptarmigan Creek above Ptarmigan Falls. This is a good place to rest and take in the scenery. Hike 200 feet farther to a trail junction; stay left for Iceberg Lake. The trail swings west below Ptarmigan Wall, then angles south. The stream below is Iceberg Creek. You climb another 500 feet, without switchbacks, in these next 2.2 miles. The environment becomes more alpine with striking floral displays. The small white spots you see on the Ptarmigan Wall might be lingering snow or mountain goats. You have hiked 4.4 miles from the trailhead when you reach Iceberg Creek. The next 0.3 mile traverses glacial rubble into a cirque filled with low-growing subalpine fir trees and flower-strewn meadows. The trail ends at a tree-lined and rocky shore. Watch your daypacks. The ground squirrels are accustomed to investigating hiker's belongings.

Iceberg is a fitting name for the lake. It stays cold due to the wall of 3,000-foot cliffs that block direct sunlight. If you arrive before July, the lake may still be frozen. Even in late summer, chunks of ice float in the milky-blue pool. Give yourself plenty of time to complete the return hike in daylight, and make noise as you go down the trail to avoid surprising any bears.

6. The Bear's Hump – Waterton

Level of difficulty: Strenuous
Duration: 1 hour
Distance: 1 mile round-trip
Elevation change: 738 feet
Best time of the year: Late July to October
Trailhead: The trail starts from the parking lot of the Waterton Visitor Resource Centre on the west side of Highway 5 across from the entrance road to the Prince of Wales Hotel.

Hiking directions: The trail is well marked, beginning next to the handicap parking space at the Wateron Visitor Resource Centre.

Special note: Take water, a snack, and your camera. The Bear's Hump provides the best views of the Waterton Valley.

The hike: The Bear's Hump is a short but taxing climb, and is tough on your knees coming back down. The staircase climb ends on a dome that greets you with an imposing panorama of the prairies to the north, Upper and Lower Waterton valleys, Waterton Townsite, and 10,466-foot Mount Cleveland, the tallest summit in Waterton–Glacier International Peace Park.

Although strenuous, this short hike gives you the feeling of accomplishment and being on the top of the world.

7. Crypt Lake – Waterton

Duration: 6 to 7 hours
Distance: 10.7 miles round-trip
Elevation change: 2,200 feet
Difficulty: Moderate to strenuous
Best time of the year: Early July through September

Trailhead: You reach the trailhead at Crypt Landing after a 20-minute boat ride from the marina in Waterton Township.

Hiking directions: There is only one trail from Crypt Landing. At 0.25 mile, you arrive at a junction to Hell Roaring Falls. Continue to Crypt Lake and visit Hell Roaring Falls on your return, if you have time.

Special note: A shuttle boat departs the marina twice each morning during the busy season. There are only two pick-up times at Crypt Landing, usually at 4 p.m. and 5 p.m. You must be in above-average shape to do this hike.

The hike: This hike includes a boat ride; startling panoramas; a 4-foot wide, 65-foot-long tunnel; a perilous ledge with handrail; a metal ladder; flower-blanketed meadows; waterfalls; and a stunning alpine lake. It is one of the most adventurous day hikes in the Canadian Rockies. Some hikers declare it is the best hike in Canada.

Glacier National Park.

The trail zigzags up through dense groves of Douglas-fir and lodgepole pine for the first 1.5 miles, then becomes a long, easy traverse along the base of Vimy Peak. The Hell Roaring Creek Valley comes into view, and across Upper Waterton Lake, Mount Anderson (8,831 feet) and Mount Richards (7,926 feet) are apparent. You pass Twin Falls at 2.1 miles as the valley turns toward the south. Pine forests are replaced by wide openings that in turn give way to a dense grove of spruce trees. Beyond the grove, the trail ascends a rock face toward Burnt Rock Falls. You have hiked about 3.5 miles. Above the falls you pass through meadows, and Crypt Falls comes into view to the south. The trail bends to the east and, at 4.8 miles, arrives at the Crypt Lake campsites, isolated in a grove of subalpine fir. Beyond the campsites, the trail comes to a talus slope where a ladder leads into a tunnel. You exit on a cliff face where a cable handrail assists your ascent to better footing. The trail then winds onto a ledge above the cliff and into meadows.

A spur trail leads to the spot where Hell Roaring Creek emerges from an underground passage, then plummets over the cliff. The main trail turns to the left and after another ridge arrives at Crypt Lake. Peaks envelop the lake. The southern tip of Crypt Lake is in the United States. Don't stay too long, because you have a boat to catch.

TRAIL ETIQUETTE

You may find total solitude on your hike, but chances are you will meet other hikers. For the best backcountry experience, consider the following guidelines while on the trail.

Take time to acknowledge other hikers. Say hello, and exchange information about trail conditions, wildlife, and scenery.

Lessen damage to the parks. Stay on the trail; cutting switchbacks and making shortcuts causes erosion.

Always yield to uphill hikers. Show courtesy by stepping aside, allowing hikers traveling uphill to keep their pace.

Apple cores, banana skins, and orange peels are not natural foods for native wildlife. Refrain from leaving them behind thinking that animals will appreciate the nourishment; they, in fact, are a detriment to wildlife diets. In addition, they are slow to decompose and are unsightly.

Leave no trace that you visited.

BEST BACKPACK TRIPS

Most visitors see Glacier National Park and Waterton Lakes National Park from a vehicle. To fully appreciate the parks you must go at a slower pace. Walking is best. You can experience the parks as few visitors do, by staying overnight at a backcountry campsite. The campsites are spread throughout the parks.

Almost half of Glacier's 65 backcountry campsites are included in a reservation system and can be reserved online beginning in April. Walk-in campsite permits as well as reserved site permits are available at backcountry offices in St. Mary Visitor Center; Apgar Backcountry Permit Center; Many Glacier, Two Medicine, and Polebridge ranger stations; and the Waterton Lakes National Park Visitor Reception Centre.

The following are descriptions of four of the best overnight hikes in Glacier National Park.

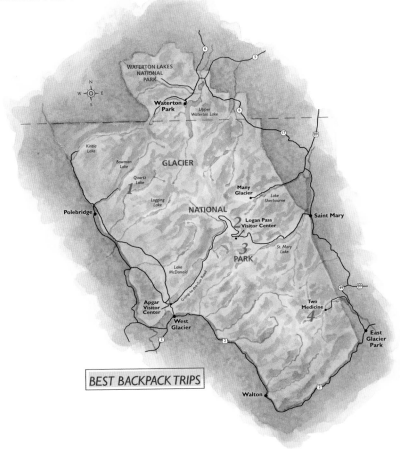

1. Quartz Lake Loop

Level of difficulty: Moderate

Distance: 12.8-mile loop

Duration: Overnight

Elevation change: 1,490 feet

Best time of the year: Late June through September

Trailhead: The trail starts south of the boat launch at Bowman Lake.

Special note: From the Camas Creek entrance on the west side of the park, follow the gravel Outside North Fork Road 21 miles to Polebridge. Get last-minute supplies at the Polebridge Mercantile, with special attention to their delicious baked goods. Reenter the park at Polebridge and follow Bowman Lake Road to Bowman Lake. Bowman Lake Road is narrow, difficult, and rocky, but passable to all automobiles. The three Quartz Lakes offer some of the best fishing in Glacier National Park.

The hike: This is a loop trail from the Bowman Lake Campground. The first 0.2 mile is along Bowman Lake. Another 0.2 mile brings you to a fork in the trail. I recommend that you hike to your left. The trail rises for the next 2.5 miles to the crest of Cerulean Ridge. The trail follows the ridgeline a short distance and then descends into the Quartz Creek drainage. The forest changes radically; you are in an area burned by the 38,000-acre Red Bench Fire of September 1988. The open landscape provides vistas of mountain peaks and ridges stretching south and west. The chain of Quartz Lakes comes into view below. As you descend, it appears that you first arrive at Middle Quartz Lake. Instead, the trail makes a turn to the east at the valley floor and arrives at Quartz Lake Campground.

The trail continues via a bridge over Quartz Creek and swings southwest past Middle Quartz Lake. A mile later is Lower Quartz Lake. The campsites at the foot of the lake are seldom used. At 9.5 miles you again cross the creek and begin a long climb over Quartz Ridge. Views from the top of the ridge include the Livingston Range to the east, and the

Apgar Mountains and the Whitefish Range to the west. The remainder of the trail is through a cool, lovely forest back to Bowman Lake.

2. Logan Pass to Many Glacier

Level of difficulty: Moderate
Distance: 15.6 miles
Duration: Overnight
Elevation change: 830 feet gain, 2,305 feet loss
Best time of the year: July through September
Trailhead: The trail begins at Logan Pass, across the Going-to-the-Sun Road, from the visitor center.

Special note: This is a hike from Logan Pass to Granite Park, then over Swiftcurrent Pass to Many Glacier. You must have transportation arranged from Many Glacier. You can reserve a walk-in site at Many Glacier Campground as part of a backcountry permit.

The hike: This is a popular route. Most of the people you encounter will be going the same direction, until you reach Granite Park, which is a hub for trails that split off in several directions.

From Logan Pass, the hike follows the Highline Trail along the Garden Wall, well above Going-to-the-Sun Road. Expect to see wildlife: bighorn sheep, mountain goats, marmots, ground squirrels, and bears. The Garden Wall is aptly named. The abundance of wildflowers is extraordinary, even into late September. Bring a wildflower identification guide.

The first 3 miles are level and easy with many small stream crossings. At 3.4 miles, you reach Haystack Butte Saddle. This is a good spot for lunch, and for views of Mount Grinnell to the north, Mount Gould to the northwest, and Haystack Butte immediately to the southwest. From the saddle, the trail traverses the Garden Wall through meadows and rock fields with little elevation change. At 3.5 miles a side trail leads to the Grinnell Glacier Overlook. This trail is 0.8 mile, and considered strenuous. A great view of the glacier is at the terminus. From this trail junction, it is another 0.8 mile to Granite Park Chalet, the campground (another mile away), and trails leading to Swiftcurrent Pass.

Swiftcurrent Pass (7,195 feet) is 1.8 miles from the Granite Park campground. The pass is at the Continental Divide and the descent into the Swiftcurrent Valley is steep, dropping 2,000 feet in the next 3.5 miles.

From the pass, the trail goes through small meadows before coming to a cliff face. Stretched before you is the Swiftcurrent Valley with its chain of lakes. The trail crisscrosses the cliff. Numerous waterfalls from Swiftcurrent Glacier will entertain you as you hike. An hour walk brings you to a grassy mound above Bullhead Lake. Once you reach the lake, the major part of your descent is over. You now walk around Bullhead Lake, pass an unnamed lake, skirt Redrock Falls, and arrive at Redrock Lake and Fishercap Lake. The area becomes increasingly forested with stands of pine trees and groves of aspen. The trail ends at Swiftcurrent Motor Lodge near Many Glacier Campground.

3. *Jackson Glacier Overlook to Lake McDonald*

Level of difficulty: Difficult

Distance: 21.5 miles

Duration: Overnight

Elevation change: 3,287-foot gain to Lincoln Pass, then 3,787-foot loss to Lake McDonald

Best time of the year: Mid-July through September

Trailhead: The hike can be done east to west, or the

National Park Service.

reverse. This description is from the east. The trailhead is at the east end of the Jackson Glacier Overlook, along the Going-to-the-Sun Road, 5 miles east of Logan Pass.

Special note: This is a very popular trail. The campsites fill quickly, so make your reservations early. Possible campsites to stay at from east to west are Reynolds Creek, Gunsight Lake, Lake Ellen Wilson, and Sperry Chalet campground. With this route you are able to rely on the shuttle, but be sure to finish the hike by 4:00 p.m. or 4:30 p.m. if you need to make it back via shuttle to the east side. Last pick up at Logan is at 7:00 p.m. going down, and there is often a waiting line for the buses.

The hike: The hike begins with a 1.5-mile descent into the valley and an intersection with the St. Mary Trail near Deadwood Falls. Turn right onto the trail toward Gunsight Lake and Pass. The trail follows the St. Mary River as it winds through moist forests and wide marshlands. Near the 4-mile mark, the trail begins a traverse along the margins of Fusillade Mountain. Gunsight Lake and campground are located at 6.2 miles. To continue, you must cross the lake outlet and climb through alpine tundra on the north face of Mount Jackson toward 6,946-foot Gunsight Pass. From here your knees will be happy that you brought your hiking poles as the trail drops away toward Lake Ellen Wilson, only 1.7 miles away. Some backpackers declare that Lake Ellen Wilson campground is the best backcountry site in the park. You leave the Lake Ellen Wilson cirque and begin an ascent along the side of Gunsight Mountain until you reach 7,050-foot Lincoln Pass, the highest point of your hike. It is all downhill from here, with your next stop in Glacier Basin, where you find Sperry campground and Sperry Chalet. You have now covered 13.7 miles. The remainder of the hike is a challenging descent along Sprague Creek and Snyder Creek. You have hiked over 21 miles of mountain landscape when you reach Lake McDonald Lodge.

4. Dawson-Pitamakan Loop

Level of difficulty: Moderate

Distance: 18.8 miles

Duration: Overnight

Elevation change: 2,935 feet gain and loss

Best time of the year: July through September

Trailhead: The North Shore Trailhead is at the end of Loop A in Two Medicine Campground.

Photo by Sam Simpson.

Special note: A ride aboard the historic tour boat *Sinopah* the length of Two Medicine Lake eliminates 2 miles of hiking. Expect wind along the ridgelines, and snow on the trail before and after Pitamakan Pass.

The hike: The North Shore Trail traverses avalanche chutes and a forest of lodgepole pine, Douglas-fir, subalpine fir, black cottonwood, alder, and aspen. The understory is dense. This is bear country. Make your presence known.

You pass the head of the lake and continue to a junction that leads you to Dawson Pass to the right and the South Shore Trail to the left. A short diversion along this trail brings you to Twin Falls. This is a good place to relax and have a snack. The trail to the pass is taxing.

A gradual ascent along Dawson Pass Trail brings you to Bighorn Basin, with its verdant meadows and scattered subalpine fir stands. No

Name Lake Trail angles to the south 1.7 miles from the South Shore Trail/Dawson Pass junction. You may have chosen the campground at No Name for your overnight. If not, begin your climb to Dawson Pass.

The next 2 miles climb 1,200 feet. The vistas at the pass include the Nyack Creek Valley to the south, and climbable Flinsch Peak to the northeast. You are now traversing the west side of Flinsch Peak and paralleling the Continental Divide; look for bighorn sheep. Another 2 miles and you reach Pitamakan Overlook, presenting a splendid panorama north and west. The trail becomes a gentle descent to Pitamakan Pass. Along the way, you meet the Cut Bank Pass Trail into the Nyack region, and Pitamakan Pass Trail into the Cut Bank Creek Valley.

The next 2 miles are steep switchbacks descending to Oldman Lake and its popular overnight campsites. You pass rocky outcroppings, with subalpine fir trees and wildflowers growing wherever there is soil. The view to the south is the horn of Flinsch Peak, and the east view is dominated by massive Rising Wolf Mountain. The Oldman Lake campsites are set in a stand of whitebark pines. The final leg of this loop contours around the base of Rising Wolf to reach Two Medicine, a gentle descent down the Dry Creek drainage. You will pass through a gully almost exclusively composed of red argillite, and through the effects of the Dry Fork Fire of 1925, to the creek's riparian bottomland. Bears inhabit this area. You may hear the songs of white-crowned sparrows, vireos, and warblers on the way to Two Medicine Campground.

BEST BICYCLE RIDES

In Glacier National Park, bicycles are restricted to roadways and designated bike routes, and are not allowed on trails. In Waterton Lakes National Park, several trails are open to bicycles. Cyclists must obey all traffic rules.

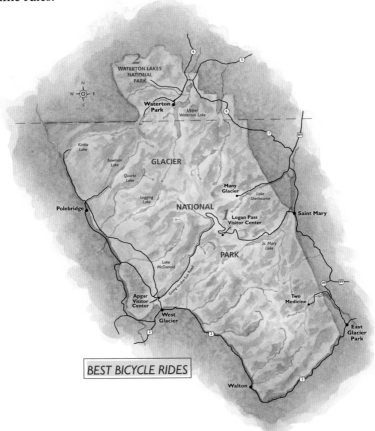

BEST BICYCLE RIDES

1. Going-to-the-Sun Road

The most popular bicycle ride in Glacier is from the Avalanche Creek Picnic Area (15.8 miles) or The Loop (7.4 miles) to Logan Pass. Each summer day, dozens of cyclists make the journey to the top, then either return to their starting point or ride down the other side of the pass, completing their trip on the opposite side of the park.

Insiders know that the absolute best bicycle ride is to climb Logan Pass under a full moon. During those times, locals gear up at Jackson Glacier Overlook, on the east side of Going-to-the-Sun Road, or The

Loop on the west. Wear reflective clothing. Use a mountain bike with low gearing. The wide tires can be deflated slightly at the pass for more rolling resistance, slowing your descent. Time your ascent to reach Logan Pass when the moon reaches its zenith.

2. Snowshoe Trail–Waterton ˅

Of Waterton Lakes National Park's many trails, four are open to bicycles. The terrain is varied and thrilling.

The best all-around trail that can be ridden by the casual cyclist is the 10.2-mile round-trip Snow-

Chuck Haney Photography.

shoe Trail. The Snowshoe Trailhead is well marked at the Red Rock Canyon parking lot at the upper end of Red Rock Parkway.

The trail is wide and rolling with moderate challenges, including creek fords. The trail intersects several hiking trails closed to bicycles, so bring your lock if you plan to explore further on foot.

BEST HORSEBACK RIDES

What it was like to see Glacier National Park before 1933? It is hard to imagine how the area appeared before tourists began using automobiles to see the park. Going-to-the-Sun Road changed the way visitors interacted with the park. Tour buses and automobiles began funneling along a single winding ribbon of road, and people came to the park for the express purpose of seeing it from a vehicle.

A horseback ride offers you a sense of early-day adventures, traversing rocky passes, meadows, and forests on mild-mannered steeds. Which rides are the best? It depends on your riding ability and how long you want to be in the saddle. For information on prices and reservations, see the Resources section at the back of this book.

BEST HORSEBACK RIDES

Easy One- to Three-Hour Rides

Depart from Apgar, West Glacier, and Lake McDonald.

Also ask about the "Cowboy Cookout" and other dinner rides from West Glacier.

All-Day Rides

Depart from Many Glacier to Poia Lake or Cracker Lake.

Whichever ride you choose, all of them allow you to contemplate what it was like touring the park in its early years. That is something that few of today's visitors experience.

Photo courtesy of Swan Mountain Outfitters.

BEST BOAT TOURS

With so many lakes and streams, Glacier and Waterton Lakes national parks are very much "water parks." A boat ride is an excellent way to see

the park from a unique vantage point. Several concessionaries offer water travel within and along park boundaries. Traveling by water can be so much fun that visitors often take multiple trips during their vacation. For reservations, see the Resources section at the back of this book.

David Restivo, National Park Service.

Best Boat Tours in Glacier

Glacier Park Boat Company provides scenic opportunities to see the park from perspectives you cannot glimpse from the roadways. The captains narrate these relaxing tours, explaining Glacier National Park's natural and cultural heritage. Boats depart from Lake McDonald Lodge, Many Glacier Hotel, Lake Josephine, Rising Sun, and Two Medicine. For the best of the best, take one of the following tours.

I. St. Mary Lake

St. Mary is the most pictur-esque of Glacier National Park's big lakes, surrounded by soaring mountains and dense forests. From late June through early September, boat tours leave Rising Sun boat dock every two hours for 1.5-hour cruises. From the comfort of the *Joy II* and *Little Chief*, you'll enjoy

Gabriel Morrow, National Park Service.

views of Sexton Glacier, several waterfalls, Wild Goose Island, and the park's rugged skyline. An optional unguided 15-minute walk to Baring Falls is offered on each tour. Also, two daily tours offer an optional 3-mile round-trip guided hike to St. Mary Falls.

2. Two Medicine Lake

David Restivo, National Park Service.

A cruise on Two Medicine Lake is rewarding in itself. But the real treat comes when you disembark at the head of the lake and hike into Glacier National Park's backcountry. Pack a lunch and plan to catch a return trip on a later boat. Riding on the 49-passenger *Sinopah* shaves 6 miles of walking off your round-trip hike to one of several possible day hike destinations. The most popular of these is Upper Two Medicine Lake at the base of 8,538-foot Mount Helen. Other options include the Dawson Pass Trail into Bighorn Basin and No Name Lake, or the Two Medicine Pass Trail south to Rockwell

Falls. From early June through early September, 45-minute boat tours leave from the Two Medicine dock four times daily.

Best Boat Tour in Waterton

3. Waterton Lake

Consider a unique two-country experience: a cruise aboard the *M. V. International* on Upper Waterton Lake. The classic 1927 ship escorts you on a grand 2-hour cruise past waterfalls, towering peaks, and across the world's longest unguarded international border to Goat Haunt, the northern gateway to Glacier National Park. Pack a lunch for the half-hour layover at Goat Haunt. Cruises leave from the marina in Waterton Townsite from May through early October, weather permitting.

David Restivo, National Park Service.

BEST PLACES TO RAFT, KAYAK, CANOE, AND BOAT

Several rafting companies near West Glacier provide half-day and full-day adventures on the Middle and North Forks of the Flathead River. Both rivers are designated Wild and Scenic and are managed by Glacier National Park and Flathead National Forest. The Middle Fork offers some exciting whitewater, while the North Fork is slower moving. Rugged scenery and whitewater define the Middle Fork from Moccasin Creek to West Glacier, following the southern boundary of the park. A half-day trip on this section is the best high-adventure water fun in the Glacier National Park area.

Within the park, you have several options for kayaking, canoeing, and boating. High-speed boats are prohibited, as are wave-runners and jet skis. Your personal boat must undergo a free inspection for non-native hitchhikers like quagga mussels and watermilfoil, an aquatic plant. Invasive animals and plants have fouled lakes across the United States, upsetting their natural balance. We must keep them out of the lakes in Glacier and Waterton Lakes.

The best lakes to kayak, canoe, and boat on are Lake McDonald, Swiftcurrent, and Two Medicine. Keep in mind that the water is cold, and winds can quickly generate large waves and unsafe conditions. You can rent watercraft equipped with life vests at Apgar, Lake McDonald, Two Medicine, and Many Glacier (see map on page 51). A leisurely half-day on any of these lakes will provide memories you will long cherish.

Perhaps the very best place to rent a canoe, rowboat, or paddleboat is Cameron Lake, at the end of the spectacular Akamina Parkway in Waterton Lakes National Park. Early morning calm water allows you to experience the serenity of one of the most remarkable places in both parks. If you are an experienced paddler, head to the south end, where you cross into the United States and Glacier National Park, and where binoculars are not needed to inspect the mountain slopes for grizzly bears.

BEST LARGE LAKES, WATERFALLS, AND OTHER FEATURES

Glacier has 762 lakes covering about 43 square miles, and 561 streams that, if stretched end-to-end, would extend from Logan Pass to Houston, Texas. These majestic valley lakes, sublime cirque lakes, streams, and waterfalls are the legacy of ice age glaciation.

Bowman Lake, Lake McDonald, St. Mary Lake, and Upper and Lower Two Medicine Lakes each fill an imprint left by valley glaciers. They are long, narrow, and are oriented east to west. Grinnell Lake, in the Many Glacier area, is an example of a cirque lake. It formed in a basin that remained after a mountain glacier melted.

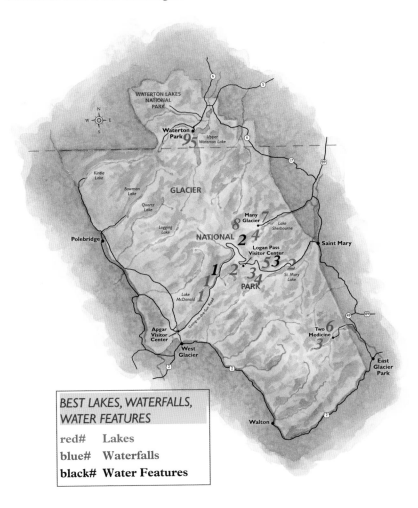

BEST LAKES, WATERFALLS, WATER FEATURES

red#   Lakes
blue#   Waterfalls
black# Water Features

Glacier's best easily accessible water features include Lake McDonald, St. Mary Lake, Two Medicine Lake, Swiftcurrent Lake, the Weeping Wall, McDonald Creek, Sacred Dancing Cascade, McDonald Falls, Sunrift Gorge, Bird Woman Falls, Running Eagle Falls, Redrock Falls, Swiftcurrent Falls, St. Mary Falls, Virginia Falls, and Baring Falls. See all of them during your visit.

Best Large Lakes

1. Lake McDonald

An old Kootenai name for the general area is translated as "Sacred Dancing." It is the largest lake in Glacier at 10 miles long, over 1 mile wide, and 472 feet deep.

Gabriel Morrow, National Park Service.

2. St. Mary Lake

Glacier's second largest lake is 9.9 miles long and 300 feet deep. It is not the most relaxing place to swim because its temperature rarely exceeds 50°F. A very cold winter can form ice up to 4 feet thick. St. Mary Lake is popular for a sunset cruise aboard one of the concessionaire's tour boats.

3. Two Medicine Lake

Bounded by Rising Wolf Mountain to the north, Sinopah Mountain to the west, and Appistoki Peak to the south, Two Medicine Lake is one of the most scenic lakes in the park. A bustling chalet area before the completion of Going-to-the-Sun

Road, Two Medicine today provides off-the-beaten-path tranquility. Sit on the east shoreline in the evening and watch the sunset over Mount Helen and return in the early morning when the water reflects towering clouds and mountains to the west. Popular day hikes from here include Aster Park, Scenic Point, Upper Two Medicine Lake, and Twin Falls.

4. Swiftcurrent Lake

Sit on the balcony or at one of the viewing windows in the Many Glacier Hotel and take in the primordial beauty of Swiftcurrent Lake's location. Either vantage point offers stunning scenery that includes the lake surrounded by lofty mountains and the skyline of the Continental Divide. Moose frequent the marshy shoreline along the lake's northwest end. Look to your right on the flanks of Altyn Peak and Mount Henkel for bears feeding on huckleberries. Gaze to your left and take in the view up the valley to Grinnell Glacier.

5. Waterton Lakes

The centerpiece lakes of Alberta's namesake park form a chain of three lakes. Upper and Middle Waterton Lakes are connected by a narrows, locally known as the Bosporus, below the Prince of Wales Hotel. Lower Waterton Lake is about 2 miles downstream from the outlet of the middle lake, bordered partly by Highway 5, and is the smallest of the three. Though not as scenic, the lower lake is a good place to see beaver, waterfowl (including swans), and an occasional bear or moose. Also, an overlook interpretive sign tells about John "Kootenai" Brown, and a nearby trail leads to his well-groomed gravesite. Upper Waterton Lake stretches more than 11 miles north to south, spanning the U.S.–Canada border. Boat tours from Waterton Townsite to Goat Haunt at the southern end of the lake feature a natural history talk and excellent views of mountains, waterfalls, and wildlife.

Best Waterfalls

Spring and early summer snowmelt sends water cascading over ledges and creates countless seasonal waterfalls. Cataracts at first, they become less impressive by mid-summer, with many reduced to a trickle or completely dried up. Several waterfalls are fed year-round by permanent snowfields and glacial melt. Some of the most impressive falls require long hikes or are inaccessible by trail. A few can be seen from the roadways or by short walks. Glacier National Park's best waterfalls to see by car or short walk include McDonald Falls, Bird Woman Falls, St. Mary Falls, Virginia Falls, Baring Falls, Running Eagle Falls, Swiftcurrent Falls, and Redrock Falls. You can see all of these during a two-day park visit.

Photo by Paul Zeller.

1. McDonald Falls

View McDonald Falls after a short walk from the Johns Lake Trailhead, 1.5 miles northeast of Lake McDonald Lodge along the Going-to-the-Sun Road. From the trailhead, cross the road and pass through the forest until the trail brings you to a bridge over North McDonald Road. Cross the bridge and locate the trail north of the road. The trail winds through a grove of cedars and hemlocks, reaching McDonald Creek in 0.25 mile. Watch for colorful harlequin ducks along this portion of the creek. McDonald Falls is the first major feature that appears. To loop back to your car, continue on the trail until you reach a bridge over the creek. The middle of the bridge provides an excellent view of Sacred Dancing Cascade, a short distance upstream. From here, proceed up to Going-to-the-Sun Road. Cross the road and follow the Johns Lake Trail back to your car.

2. Bird Woman Falls

The name refers to Sacajawea, the Shoshone woman and interpreter who assisted Lewis and Clark during the 1804–1806 Corps of Discovery expedition. Plummeting 492 feet, the falls is visible from several vantage points along Going-to-the-Sun Road west of Logan Pass. The best view is at the Bird Woman Falls turnout. Binoculars help, because even from here the waterfall is about 2 miles distant.

Photo by Greg Vaughn.

3. St. Mary Falls

A 1.5-mile easy round-trip hike takes you to a footbridge spanning the St. Mary River. The immediate area provides outstanding views of the 50-foot waterfall. The trailhead is about 0.3 mile west of Sunrift Gorge along the Going-to-the-Sun Road. Follow the trail to the valley floor. Stay right at the Piegan Pass Trail junction.

4. Virginia Falls

If you are a waterfall enthusiast, you will want to see Virginia Falls after visiting St. Mary Falls. From the St. Mary River footbridge, continue on the same trail 0.5 mile to the base of Virginia Falls. Listen to the sounds as water free-falls from a 50-foot precipice and crashes into a shallow pool.

5. Baring Falls

This waterfall was once known as Water Ouzel Falls, an Old World name for a bird we now call the American dipper (see page 90). These entertaining birds are often seen near the base of the falls, walking into the water in search of insect larvae. You get to 40-foot Baring Falls from Sun Point. Travel the Going-to-the-Sun Road 7.7 miles east of Logan Pass to the Sun Point parking area. Follow the Sun Point Trail, which begins in the southeastern corner of the parking area. The easy round-trip walk is 1.4 miles.

6. Running Eagle Falls

This unique waterfall is an easy 0.3-mile round-trip walk from the parking area 1 mile west of the Two Medicine entrance station. Running Eagle Falls consists of two separate waterfalls, hence its nickname, Trick Falls. Spring runoff brings water rushing over the 40-foot top ledge, hiding a cave-like opening in the cliff face. When the upper waterfall dries up in mid-summer, the creek continues to flow into a sinkhole at the top of the cliff and out through the opening, thus creating the lower 20-foot waterfall. A sign at the parking area interprets the importance of this place to the Blackfeet Nation, and how the waterfall got its name.

7. Swiftcurrent Falls

Swiftcurrent Creek exits Swiftcurrent Lake and passes under the access road to Many Glacier Hotel. The creek crashes over and around boulders for 0.1 mile before making its vertical drop over Swiftcurrent Falls. The best place to see the waterfall is 0.2 mile east of the Many Glacier Hotel turn-off along the Many Glacier Road. A small gravel turnout on the south side provides excellent views of the waterfall with Grinnell Point as a backdrop.

8. Redrock Falls

Walk about 2.5 miles on a well-used trail to see Redrock Falls. Begin at the western end of the Swiftcurrent Store parking lot in Many Glacier. Follow the Swiftcurrent Pass Trail. At 2 miles you will reach the foot of Redrock Lake and see the waterfall another 0.5 mile ahead. Take advantage of places to photograph the falls from afar; it is not possible to photograph its entirety up close. The water from Swiftcurrent Creek flows in a series of pools and cataracts over red argillite rock. The trail parallels the falls, providing delightful angles for viewing the turbulent pools and plummeting water.

Jason Savage Photography.

9. Cameron Falls

This is the most visited and photographed spot in Waterton Lakes National Park. The falls are located on the western edge of the Waterton Townsite near the junction of Evergreen Avenue and Cameron Falls Road. A paved trail to the right leads to good viewpoints of the upper cascade.

Best Other Water Features

I. McDonald Creek and Sacred Dancing Cascade

Going-to-the-Sun Road parallels McDonald Creek from Johns Lake Trailhead to Logan Creek. McDonald Creek is the most spectacular watercourse in the park. The water rushes through chutes, flows through

deep reflecting pools, takes abrupt 90-degree turns, and sparkles like multi-faceted diamonds as it tumbles over rocky outcrops.

Several turnouts along the Going-to-the-Sun Road between Johns Lake Trailhead and Logan Creek allow access to the creek and views of the surrounding mountains. Two that I recommend are Red Rock Point, 0.75 mile north of Avalanche Creek, and McDonald Creek Overlook, 1.5 miles south of Avalanche Creek.

2. Weeping Wall

National Park Service.

Snowmelt and runoff flows over the ground and from springs coming up through the rock layers of Haystack Butte below the Garden Wall. The road cut resulting from the construction of Going-to-the-Sun Road created the Wall's waterfall effect. Make sure that your car windows are rolled up if you decide to drive near the cascade. The early summer deluge can flood your car in an instant.

3. Sunrift Gorge

Every park visitor should see Sunrift Gorge, located 10.4 miles west of St. Mary and 100 feet from Going-to-the-Sun Road. Baring Creek cuts through a narrow rock fracture and produces a deep gorge filled with clear, rushing, cold water from the Sexton Glacier area.

BEST PLACES TO FISH

From the earliest days of Glacier National Park, people tried to change the park to fulfill their wishes. Park employees hunted mountain lions, grizzly bears, and wolves to protect deer and elk. Streams and lakes were stocked so that anglers would find fish in abundance.

Photo by Linda Duvanich.

Until 1971, fish were raised in hatcheries outside the park and relocated in park waters. Many of these fish species, which now exist in

BEST PLACES TO FISH
red# Lakes
blue# Streams

large numbers, came from Minnesota, New York, and even Yellowstone National Park.

Some lakes and streams continue to support native fish populations that have thrived here since the last ice age 10,000 years ago. The park now manages fish populations for their role in the ecosystem rather than for their sport value. The best-known species of native fish are the westslope cutthroat trout, mountain whitefish, and bull trout. **Bull trout are listed as threatened under the Endangered Species Act; any bull trout caught must be released immediately.** Protection of bull trout is also strictly enforced in Waterton Lakes National Park. Get fishing regulations at the Waterton Visitor Resource Centre on the west side of Highway 5 across from the entrance road to the Prince of Wales Hotel.

Within Glacier, there are 1,557 miles of streams, 131 named lakes, and 69 unnamed lakes. Many of the streams are shallow and barren, and most of the lakes are nutrient-poor and too cold to support fish. At least 50 lakes and 18 streams have trout or whitefish. Of these, 9 lakes and 3 streams offer the best opportunities for successful fishing.

No fishing license or permit is needed to fish inside Glacier National Park. However, the park does enforce regulations designed to protect native fish. Ask at a visitor center for this year's regulations before you fish. Also, see the Resources section at the back of this book for online information on fishing in the park.

Best Lake Fishing

1. Quartz Lake Chain

A 6-mile hike from Bowman Lake Campground, Quartz Lake holds cutthroat trout and bull trout. You can also reach Middle Quartz Lake and Lower Quartz Lake via the Quartz Lake loop trail. This is wild, beautiful country, with deep forests and great vistas; bring your camera. Middle Quartz Lake is immediately downstream from Quartz Lake. It holds cutthroat trout and bull trout.

Lower Quartz Lake is the third lake on the loop trail from Bowman Lake Campground. The lake has cutthroat trout, bull trout, and whitefish. Quartz Lake, Middle Quartz Lake, and Lower Quartz Lake can all be fished during a long day hike, or as part of a multi-day backpacking adventure. A backcountry permit is required for any overnight stays.

2. Harrison Lake

Harrison Lake is home to cutthroat trout and bull trout. The trailhead is 10 miles east of West Glacier on U.S. Highway 2. Wait until mid-July to ford the Middle Fork of the Flathead River, and skip this trip if the river is high. After crossing the river, hike 3 miles to the foot of the lake.

3. Trout Lake

Aptly named Trout Lake is known for cutthroat trout. From the trailhead at the Lake McDonald Ranger Station, the West Lakes Trail climbs moderately to a saddle between Howe Ridge and Mount Stanton, reaching the lake in 4 miles.

4. Bullhead Lake

Near the head of the Swiftcurrent Valley, Bullhead Lake offers good fishing for brook trout. From the western end of the Swiftcurrent Motor Inn parking lot, hike 6.5 miles west on the Swiftcurrent Pass Trail. You will also pass Fishercap Lake and Redrock Lake, both considered fair for brook trout. Bears and moose frequent this area.

5. Otokomi Lake

The 6-mile hike from the Rising Sun Store to Otokomi Lake is moderately difficult, gaining almost 1,900 feet. The lake holds cutthroat trout, some very large. Otokomi Lake is ringed by red argillite cliffs. The outlet area is covered by krummholz groves of subalpine fir. The rocks and trees provide a spectacular setting. One August, I found the outlet clogged with trout, reminiscent of a fish hatchery.

6. Two Medicine Lake

Two Medicine Lake offers easy access. You can fish for brook trout and rainbow trout anywhere along the shore, or, from June through early September, rent a boat from the concessionaire. Few places on Earth can match this beautiful setting for angling.

7. Upper Two Medicine Lake

You can reach Upper Two Medicine Lake either by hiking 5.5 miles from Two Medicine Campground, or by taking a boat ride to the head of Two Medicine Lake, which shaves 3 miles off the trip each way. The upper lake has brook trout and rainbow trout. Also watch for osprey, mule deer, and bears.

Best Stream Fishing

1. Bowman Creek Below Bowman Lake

From Bowman Lake to Polebridge and the confluence with the North Fork of the Flathead River, Bowman Creek holds cutthroat trout. This is one of the few places you might see a gray wolf. Note that the reach of Bowman Creek above the lake is closed to fishing.

2. Lower McDonald Creek

The outlet creek below Lake McDonald is designated as a "fishing for fun" catch-and-release area, where only single-hook, artificial lures may be used. Cutthroat, whitefish, rainbow trout, and brook trout are the sought-after species.

3. Belly River

Hike from the trailhead at the U.S.–Canada border crossing on MT Highway 17 (Chief Mountain Highway). Rainbow trout and grayling are two popular fish species here. This is moose and black bear country. The North Fork of the Belly River, which empties into Alberta and the Blood Timber Reserve, is closed to fishing to protect bull trout.

> **FISH FOES**
> *Non-native fish destroy native fish populations by:*
> • *Preying on them.*
> • *Outcompeting them for food.*
> • *Bringing diseases that native fish cannot resist.*
> • *Interbreeding with native fish.*
> • *Outnumbering them in lakes, rivers, or streams.*

BEST HISTORIC SITES

Glacier National Park is home to 350 buildings and sites that are listed on the National Register of Historic Places. Among the sites are Going-to-the-Sun Road, Lake McDonald Lodge, Glacier Park Lodge, Two Medicine Store, Many Glacier Hotel, Sperry Chalet, Granite Park Chalet, Belton Chalet, several Great Northern Railway buildings, some ranger stations, patrol cabins, fire lookouts, and concession facilities. Stories of the building of the historic hotels and chalets are shared in Ray Djuff and Chris Morrison's comprehensive book *Glacier's Historic Hotels & Chalets: View with a Room.*

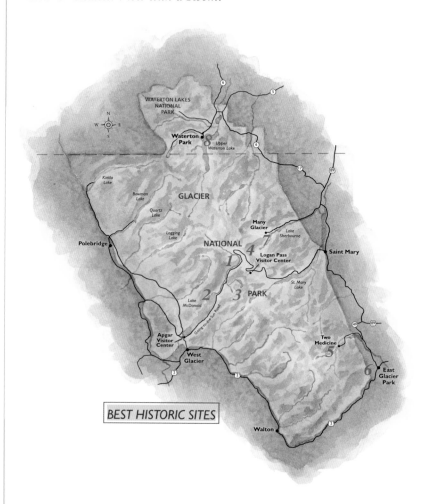

1. Going-to-the-Sun Road

Going-to-the-Sun Road is an enthralling 50-mile engineering wonder. Built between 1920 and 1932, it is also a Historic Civil Engineering

Landmark. It is designed to expose fantastic vistas with limited impact on the landscape. The road passes through the core of the park, hugging canyon walls and twisting over the Continental Divide at 6,646-foot Logan Pass. Many visitors come to Glacier for the sole purpose of touring this spectacular road.

2. Lake McDonald Lodge

The road reached the lodge in 1922, eight years after the lodge opened. Before then, visitors arrived by boat. Owner John Lewis modeled the interior after a hunting inn. Some of his taxidermy mounts still adorn the lobby. The Swiss-style chalet exterior mirrored the construction design of the Great Northern Railway park buildings. Its architecture, unique interior, and age enhance its charm.

3. Sperry Chalet

The Sperry Chalet complex was built by the railroad to provide tourists easy access to Sperry Glacier and to entice tourists from staying at rival Lake McDonald Lodge. The dining room was built in 1913, and the two-story hotel opened in 1914. Italian

Photo by Miranda Leftridge.

stonemasons constructed both of native rock. Testament to their work is that both buildings are little changed even with decades of extreme alpine conditions. The chalet continues to operate, with seventeen guest rooms and the dining room. You must walk or ride horseback to reach the chalet.

Photo by Bruce Dellard.

4. Granite Park Chalet

Accessible only by trail, Granite Park Chalet was built in 1914 and 1915 by the Great Northern Railway for backcountry accommodations along their North Circle Tour. The tour connected the Going-to-the-Sun Chalet, Granite Park Chalet, and Many Glacier Hotel. The highest chalet in the park at 6,690 feet, Granite Park prompted Great Northern to advertise, "Be prepared for rain, high winds, and freezing temperatures at any time."

5. Two Medicine Store

Originally constructed in 1915 as the dining hall, it is the only remaining building of the Two Medicine Chalet complex. President Franklin Roosevelt made a radio broadcast here on August 5, 1934. During his talk—not one of his famous official "Fireside Chats"—he declared, "I wish every American, both old and young, could have been with me today. The great mountains, the glacier, the lakes and the trees make me long to stay for the rest of the summer." He left the next morning.

6. Glacier Park Lodge

In 1912, the Great Northern Railway built Glacier Park Lodge as the gateway hotel to the park. In the early years, members of the Blackfeet

Nation met tourists arriving on the *Oriental Limited*. Visitors found lodge employees clad in a mixture of Western, oriental, and Swiss attire. The lobby echoed these themes with animal mounts, totem poles, and oriental lanterns. Great Northern president Louis Hill understood good customer service. The Glacier Park Lodge experience was meant to elevate the visitor's anticipation and foreshadow the excitement awaiting them while they explored the Shining Mountains and stayed at the company's lodgings within the park.

7. Many Glacier Hotel

The *See America First* campaign encouraged tourism at home rather than abroad. Many Glacier Hotel's Swiss-inspired architecture provided

an attractive European flavor. Opened July 4, 1915, and completed in 1918, the Great Northern Railway declared it "one of the most noteworthy hotels that ever has been erected in America." Today you can relax on the expansive porch or at one of the viewing galleries and enjoy the reflection of the encompassing cloud-piercing mountains in Swiftcurrent Lake.

8. Prince of Wales Hotel

The Great Northern Railway built this hotel in 1927 to attract tourists from the United States. Travelers could choose a vacation package that began in East or West Glacier and combine a variety of hotels, lodges, and tent camps, ending their trip with a ride aboard the *M. V. International* from Goat Haunt to Waterton. The Prince of Wales Hotel was their last

Chuck Haney Photography.

major overnight stay before going back to Glacier National Park by bus. Designed for the "affluent tourist," a one-week all-inclusive ticket was more than $1,000, about equal to the average family's annual income at the time.

Located on a hilltop with a commanding view of Waterton Townsite, the Prince of Wales is one of the largest wooden buildings in Alberta and has National Historic Site status. Visit the impressive lobby and enjoy the floor-to-ceiling windows with a breathtaking view all the way to Glacier's Goat Haunt at the far end of the lake.

ROOSEVELT'S TREE ARMY: THE CCC IN GLACIER

One of President Franklin Roosevelt's first moves after taking office in 1933 was the formation of the Civilian Conservation Corps (CCC), also known as "Roosevelt's Tree Army." Facing a nation on the brink of economic disaster, the president's mission was to revive the country by employing thousands of young men to preserve America's natural and cultural heritage. Teams of men worked on projects to build the nation's rural infrastructure and reclaim despoiled landscapes.

Photo courtesy Glacier National Park.

The CCC played a major role between 1933 and 1942 in developing Glacier National Park. Almost 1,300 CCC enrollees worked on reforestation, campground development, trail construction, fire hazard reduction, and fire fighting. For example, in the Apgar area they removed snags from the 1929 fire, graded roads, built trails, and cleared the campsites you might be using today.

BEST WILDLIFE

Glacier National Park has more than 70 native mammals. Except for caribou and bison, all of the species that were here 500 years ago are present today. The park is famous for celebrated iconic animals, such as mountain goats and grizzly bears. Other mammals are common though less renowned, and a few are notable but rarely seen.

Mammal Checklist

Many of the 70 species of mammals in Glacier National Park are abundant. You may encounter about 20. Start a checklist. It could require several visits to the park to see all of these animals, giving you an excuse to return often.

KEEP WILDLIFE WILD AND HEALTHY

Birds and squirrels that live around picnic areas and campgrounds have learned that people leave bits and pieces of food behind. Because the animals are cute and entertaining, some people feed them.

Feeding wildlife leads to problems, though. First, the animals become dependent on handouts, an easy source of food. Also, they become a nuisance around picnic areas and campgrounds, and could carry diseases that can be contracted by humans. Finally, when animals become dependent on handouts, they tend to ignore the food they can get from the wild. Human food is meant for people. It does not provide the necessary nutrients for wildlife to survive. Animals that rely on human food may become malnourished and unable to survive the winter. Keep your picnic area and campsite clean, and remember, do not feed the animals.

___ Beaver
___ Bighorn sheep
___ Black bear
___ Chipmunk
___ Columbian ground squirrel
___ Coyote
___ Elk
___ Flying squirrel
___ Golden-mantled ground squirrel
___ Gray wolf
___ Grizzly bear
___ Hoary marmot
___ Moose
___ Mountain goat
___ Mountain lion
___ Mule deer
___ Pika
___ Red squirrel
___ White-tailed deer
___ Wolverine

Chipmunk

Least *(Tamias minimus)*
Red-tailed *(Tamias ruficaudus)*
Yellow-pine *(Tamias amoenus)*

National Park Service.

Chipmunks are affable squirrels. Few sights are more charming than a chipmunk sitting on a rock with forepaws folded against its chest, or holding a flower to its mouth.

The genus *Tamias* is Greek for "storer." They do not build fat like ground squirrels, so chipmunks hoard food in underground caches for hibernation. Their periods of dormancy can last from many days to several weeks. They awaken often during winter and feed on their larder. Hibernation ends in April with little weight loss.

The three species in Glacier National Park are almost impossible to distinguish by sight. It is more reliable to identify chipmunks by habitat. Least chipmunks live in alpine meadows, talus slopes, and tundra environments. Red-tailed chipmunks live in rock outcroppings up to timberline. Yellow-pine chipmunks are abundant in the brushy areas of the lower elevations, as well as in rocky places and open forests.

Not by their choosing, chipmunks play an important role as prey for many mammals and birds. If they avoid predators, they can live up to 6 years in the park.

Best Places to See Chipmunks:

Look for yellow-pine chipmunks in campgrounds, and around buildings in St. Mary, Many Glacier, Cut Bank, Apgar Village, and Two Medicine. You will find red-tailed chipmunks at Sun Point and the many turnouts along Going-to-the-Sun Road between The Loop and Wild Goose Island turnout. Find least chipmunks at Logan Pass, Oberlin Bend, and the Highline Trail.

Golden-mantled Ground Squirrel

Callospermophilus lateralis

"It's 'Chip and Dale!'" Well, yes and no. The Disney animators who drew the beloved cartoon characters must have thought that golden-mantled ground squirrels were chipmunks. They are not, but are often

National Park Service.

misidentified as chipmunks. You will see these lovable squirrels throughout Glacier National Park. They are accustomed to sharing their habitat with humans, and are common denizens in campgrounds, picnic areas, around lodges, and at scenic turnouts. Golden-mantled ground squirrels that live at high elevations enter their dens fat on seeds, insects, and bird eggs in late August. September is the time for those living in lower elevations to enter their 8-month hibernation. Their scientific name *Callospermophilus* is Greek for *kallos* "beauty," *spermatos* "seed," and *phileo*, "love."

Best Places to See Golden-mantled Ground Squirrels:

Watch for them at Two Medicine Camp Store, Sun Point, The Loop, Apgar Village, and all campgrounds and picnic areas.

Red Squirrel

Tamiasciurus hudsonicus

National Park Service.

The red squirrel is one of two tree squirrels in the park. Locally known as the pine squirrel, these tree acrobats will please you with their endearing antics. You may detect pine squirrels by sound before sight. Their noisy chattering is a territorial warning for intruders to stay away. With a home range of less than two football fields and populations of two squirrels to three acres, their territories often overlap. As with other animals, they do not like competitors and will fight to protect their food supplies. Red squirrels do not hibernate, and can live 10 years if they can avoid owls, martens, foxes, and bobcats.

Best Places to See Red Squirrels:

Red squirrels are common throughout the park in Douglas-fir and Engelmann spruce communities up to timberline.

Columbian Ground Squirrel
Urocitellus columbianus

These Rip Van Winkles range throughout the park, but are most entertaining near the Logan Pass Visitor Center as they feed on various grasses. If these squirrels seem indifferent to your presence here, it is because they are acclimated to humans and deem you no threat. Also, they are too busy feeding, storing fat for the long winter. Columbian ground squirrels hibernate up to nine months. They go underground in early August when their vegetative food supply begins to dry, and begin to emerge in mid-April. These dates vary, depending on snow depth and elevation.

Some people refer to Columbian ground squirrels as gophers. They belong, however, to a family of animals that includes marmots, chipmunks, tree squirrels, flying squirrels, and prairie dogs. The only gopher in Glacier National Park is the 6-inch-long northern pocket gopher.

Best places to see Columbian Ground Squirrels:

Look for ground squirrels at Logan Pass, Big Bend, Rising Sun, Two Medicine, Cut Bank Campground, and on the flats around St. Mary.

Northern Flying Squirrel
Glaucomys sabrinus

At the close of day, the sky begins to darken, and you settle before a campfire. Out of the corner of your eye, you spot something gliding among the trees. While you were getting ready to sleep, many animals are awakening.

The glider may have been a northern flying squirrel. Common in Glacier

National Park, and native to Montana, these squirrels have cape-like skin flaps stretching between the front and rear legs, enabling them to glide from one tree to the next. They have a glide ratio of 3, meaning that they can glide 30 feet for every 10 feet of drop; people's hang gliders come close to this ratio.

Northern flying squirrels live in the same forests as red squirrels, and, like red squirrels, do not hibernate. They snuggle with family members, staying warm in abandoned woodpecker holes on cold days. Their fur is dense, long, and soft.

Best Places to See Northern Flying Squirrels:
Look for northern flying squirrels at dusk in the wooded campgrounds, including Fish Creek, Avalanche Creek, Sprague Creek, Rising Sun, Two Medicine, Many Glacier, and Apgar.

Hoary Marmot
Marmota caligata

National Park Service.

About the size of a soccer ball, the hoary marmot is the largest member of the squirrel family. They weigh up to 20 pounds and can further be distinguished by their mock boxing matches, nuzzling of one another, sun bathing (up to 40 percent of their time on a sunny day), and loud chirping whistles. Commonly known as "Whistle Pigs," hoary marmots are at home in alpine meadows near talus slopes and krummholz forests. They spend their summers feasting on grasses, sedges, glacier lilies, paintbrush plants, and silky lupines. Glacier's marmots need copious stored fat to survive the high country winter. They hibernate in a colony of 6 to 8, in a den, under the rocks and snow for up to 34 weeks. Food deprivation and cold temperatures trigger hibernation, and they enter their dens for the final time in September.

Best Places to See Hoary Marmots:
Look for marmots at Logan Pass, Big Bend, Highline Trail, Iceberg Lake Trail, and Grinnell Glacier Trail.

National Park Service.

Pika

Ochotona princeps

Like a farmer covering haystacks in a midsummer thunderstorm, the pika stashes alpine flowers and grasses it has harvested to keep them dry. When the sun returns, the pika spreads the hay on rocks in a crosshatched pattern. The provisions are then stored deep within the rockslide for winter food. Also called rock rabbits, you will hear pikas' short bugle-like squeaks if you approach their homes. They live above timberline in talus fields that edge alpine meadows. The size of a grapefruit, with tiny ears, pikas stay active all winter among the rocks under several feet of snow.

Best Places to See Pikas:

Listen for pikas along the Hidden Lake Overlook Trail, 1.25 miles from the trailhead in the talus field on the north side of the trail. Follow the squeaks, and then sit quietly. Pikas can be seen along most high-elevation trails where boulder fields are adjacent to alpine meadows.

Beaver

Castor canadensis

Beavers are nighttime engineers. Imagine the difficulty of building a dam across a stream at night. That is what beavers can do. The sound of running water activates an instinct to stop it the only way they know—building a dam. The resulting ponds provide their immediate habitat, but beaver ponds eventually fill with silt and become meadows favored by elk, deer, bobcats, and foxes.

> **TOO PARCHED FOR PIKAS**
>
> Pikas live in a narrow temperature range. Insulated by snowpack covering their alpine homes, they can survive the winters without hibernating. But if they are exposed to summer temperatures exceeding 70 degrees for just a few hours they will perish. Global warming has affected pikas in western states, with a reduction of up to 40 percent of their habitat in some areas. Glacier's pika population adjusts to these conditions by attempting to relocate up the mountains to more hospitable climes. They have already migrated to the highest elevations in the park, with no new territory to enter.

National Park Service.

The largest American rodent, a beaver mates for life, and can measure 4 feet long and weigh 80 pounds. They can swim at Olympic free-style speeds of 5 mph and remain underwater for 15 minutes, with transparent eyelids that act like goggles. In Glacier and Waterton, beavers can live for 24 years.

Best Places to See Beaver:

The Beaver Pond Loop Trail near St. Mary is your best bet. Also watch for beaver dams, lodges, and cut trees along lowland streams.

Mule Deer

Odocoileus hemionus

Mule deer are the most common deer in Glacier National Park. They have a larger frame than white-tailed deer, with a darker coat, a black-tipped tail, and large "mule" ears. White-tailed deer trot when they run, while mule deers' bouncing gait is distinctive.

Bill Hayden, National Park Service.

Like white-tailed deer, mule deer are browsers. Where their habitats somewhat overlap, their diets vary enough that they are not in direct competition for food.

Mule deer live up to 11 years in the park if as adults they avoid mountain lions and wolves, and as fawns they are lucky enough to also avoid coyotes, eagles, bears, and bobcats.

Best Places to See Mule Deer:

Mule deer prefer open sagebrush habitats and subalpine forests. Look for them along Two Medicine Road, Many Glacier Road, Camas Road, Going-to-the-Sun Road from St. Mary to the Jackson Glacier turnout, and along the Akamina Parkway in Waterton.

White-tailed Deer
Odocoileus virginianus

National Park Service.

You will recognize white-tailed deer by their long tails, white on the underside, which they wave as a warning signal when they gallop away from danger. When needed, they can run 30 miles per hour, leap as high as 10 feet, and can cross Going-to-the-Sun Road in a single vault. They spend more than 40 percent of their day browsing on grasses, brushy plants, twigs, and leaves. White-tailed deer are common in Glacier and Waterton and can live 16 years here if they avoid wolves and mountain lions.

Best Places to See White-Tailed Deer:

White-tailed deer are a forest animal, scattered throughout the parks up to timberline.

Rocky Mountain Elk
Cervus elaphus nelsoni

National Park Service.

If you see something that looks like an oversize deer with a beige rump and legs darker than the rest of its body, you are looking at an elk. They are a member of the deer family that includes mule deer, white-tailed deer, moose, and caribou. Before Columbus arrived in the Western Hemisphere, there were more than 10 million elk in North America. Their numbers were reduced to 1 million through uncontrolled hunting and land development. Protected in both Waterton and Glacier, they can live up to 15 years, feeding on grasses, lichens, bushes, tree bark, and saplings. Wolves, bears, cougars, and occasionally wolverines prey on elk.

Elk are territorial. Both males and females use saplings to mark their territory. Males strip off bark with their antlers, and females remove bark with their teeth. They rub the saplings with their muzzles to cover the plants with scent.

Many people visit the park in autumn during mating season to listen to elk as much as see them. At dusk and dawn, bull elk "bugle," a whistle that challenges other males and attracts females into a harem.

ELK ESSENTIALS

One female dominates each herd of cows. A cow can weigh up to 500 pounds. Antlers on a 1,100-pound bull can grow up to 5 feet long and weigh 40 pounds. An elk's top two canine teeth are called ivories. Scientists believe ivories are remnants of saber-like tusks that ancestral species of elk used in combat. According to Lewis and Clark's journals, the Corps of Discovery killed and ate at least 375 elk during its three-year expedition.

Best Places to See Elk:

Summer is a difficult time to see elk because they travel in small groups in the forests. Autumn and early spring are the best times to see elk. Before winter, they migrate to lower elevations and congregate in herds. St. Mary and the North Fork areas are the best places to encounter elk.

Moose

Alces alces

How can you tell if a moose is full-grown? Measure its tail, of course. A full-grown adult moose only has a 3-inch tail!

Good luck measuring its tail; this largest member of the deer

National Park Service.

family can be irritable. Moose have been known to charge people, horses, cars, snowmobiles, road maintenance machines, and locomotives.

Moose of both sexes have a "bell," which is the flap of skin and long hair that hangs from the throat. No one knows its purpose. A bull can weigh up to 1,000 pounds and stand 5.5 feet at the shoulder. These bulls can grow majestic antlers up to 50 inches wide that weigh 60 pounds. They lose their antlers each year.

Look for moose in marshy areas and meadows during the spring and summer. You will find moose in forested areas as winter progresses.

"Moos" is an Algonquin word that means "twig-eater." An Algonquin legend says that if you dream of moose often, you will live a very long time. Pleasant dreams!

Best Places to See Moose:

Watch for moose around Kootenai Lakes, south of Goat Haunt, Beaver Pond Loop Trail, St. Mary, Fishercap Lake, the Many Glacier area, and along the first 2 miles of the Red Rock Parkway in Waterton.

> **MIGHTY MOOSE**
> *Moose have hollow hair that helps them float and swim at 6 mph for up to 2 hours. When necessary, moose can dive 20 feet under water and stay submerged for 40 seconds. They can run up to 36 mph for short distances, or as far as 15 miles without stopping. Moose have front teeth only on the bottom jaw. They eat about 40 to 60 pounds of willow, aspen, and aquatic plants a day.*

National Park Service.

Bighorn Sheep
Ovis canadensis

Imagine driving your car into a solid wall at 20 mph. Now, think of doing that repeatedly for up to 24 hours! Male bighorn sheep do something analogous to this in autumn as they pair off a few feet apart, rear up on their hind legs, and ram each other. Your car would look awful after such a pounding, but the sheep's thick, bony skulls prevent serious damage. Rams are celebrated for their large, curled horns. They represent status to the sheep and are used as weapons in battles for dominance or mating rights. Their horns can weigh 30 pounds, more than all the bones in their body. Consider lifting that weight repeatedly for hours. The thin alpine air can carry the crack of their colliding horns a mile away. The battle rages until one ram leaves.

There are about 1,000 bighorn sheep in Glacier National Park. Like mountain goats, they have split hooves and rough hoof bottoms for gripping rugged mountain surfaces. Bighorn sheep prefer less rocky terrain than goats, but this makes them more vulnerable to mountain lions, coyotes, and wolves. Golden eagles prey on lambs that are born on secluded rock ledges, ready to walk at birth. If they avoid predators, they can live up to 15 years in the park. Bighorn herds of up to 100 migrate to the park's lower meadows to forage on grasses, seeds, yarrow plants, serviceberry bushes, mountain maple trees, and sagebrush.

Best Places to See Bighorn Sheep:
Look for bighorn sheep at Logan Pass near the Hidden Lake Trail. Several live in the Waterton Townsite. They are also seen on the south face of Pollock Mountain, north of Going-to-the-Sun Road at Logan Pass. You will need binoculars.

Mountain Goat
Oreamnos americanus

The Great Northern Railway adopted the mountain goat as its marketing symbol in 1921. A trademarked depiction of a goat nicknamed *Rocky*, along with slogans like "See America First" and "The National Park Route" were intended to attract tourists to Glacier. Although not an official National Park Service symbol, over time the mountain goat became emblematic of Glacier National Park.

Mountain goats spend most of their time grazing on grasses, herbs, ferns, mosses, and lichens. When not feeding, they rest on rocky cliffs protected from predators. A sure-footed climber at high elevations, their cloven hooves can spread apart, while their inner pads provide traction to help them navigate steep rocky slopes.

Despite its common name, it is not a true goat, but is a member of the Bovidae family that includes antelope and cattle. Predation is uncommon. The young are sometimes taken by golden eagles, but only mountain lions are surefooted enough to kill adults. Even that is unlikely as mountain goats have a keen sense of smell and can visually detect movement up to a mile away. Their average lifespan in the parks is 15 years.

Best Places to See Mountain Goats:
Look for mountain goats feeding near Oberlin Bend and the first 0.25

mile of the Highline Trail from Logan Pass. Hikers find them at many of the passes above 6,000 feet and at Sperry Chalet. Goats are attracted to salt. They are sometimes observed licking nutrients left behind by peoples' hands from the wooden handrail at Hidden Lake Overlook. Finally, they congregate across the Middle Fork of the Flathead River at a location known as Goat Lick. Look for the Goat Lick Overlook 3 miles east of the Walton Ranger Station off U.S. Highway 2.

Coyote

Canis latrans

Yip, yip, yip! The coyote's scientific name means "barking dog." A chorus starts at dusk with one coyote yipping then progressing to a howl. Quickly, several more will join the song. The Song Dog of the West is numerous and inhabits every area of the park up to timberline. A scavenger and small animal hunter, coyotes are not tolerated by other predators. However, they take advantage of badgers' hunting forays. When badgers enter ground squirrel burrows to hunt spring litters, coyotes will wait at secondary tunnel entrances for fleeing squirrels.

> **ANTLERS OR HORNS?**
> Antlers are bony substances that grow on the heads of male deer, elk, and moose each year. The annual cycle of antler growth is regulated by the lengthening daylight hours in spring. New antlers are covered in fuzzy skin called velvet. Antlers harden by late summer and the velvet peels away. By September, bone-like antlers aid males during competitions of the rut or mating season. Antlers fall off in January or February and the cycle begins again.
>
> Horns are bony outgrowths on the heads of certain ungulates, including bighorn sheep and mountain goats. Both males and females have horns. Horns are never shed, but remain with the animal for life.

Photo by Linda Duvanich.

Best Places to See Coyotes: Look for coyotes hunting rodents in the grasslands north of St. Mary Lake, in the Cut Bank Creek area, and along Red Rock Parkway in Waterton. You may encounter a coyote trotting down a road in front of your car. They use our roadways, too. Remember not to feed them!

Gray Wolf
Canus lupus

National Park Service.

Gray wolves began re-colonizing Glacier National Park's North Fork Valley in the early 1980s. They were absent from the park after the 1930s due to a predator control program that began in the early days of the park. The program was phased-out in the 1950s and 1960s. Park officials believe the wolves moved down from Canada. Alone, they eat small mammals and birds; in packs they prey on deer, moose, and elk.

WOLF WAYS

Wolves walk on the tips of their toes and can run as fast as 35 mph. In Glacier, their habitat is the forest; they prey on deer and moose. There has never been a reported incident of a wolf attacking a human in the park. Wolf offspring are called pups, born in a litter of 4 to 6 inside a den (a cave or hole in the ground).

You will be lucky to see a wolf while you are in Glacier because they lead secret lives. Although you will probably not see a wolf, you can still listen for one. The howl of the gray wolf can travel 10 miles. As afternoon light fades in the North Fork Valley, listen for the long, sorrowful howl of the gray wolf. Its cry reminds you that you are visiting a true American wilderness.

A Place That You Might See a Wolf:
Your best chance to glimpse a wolf is in the North Fork Valley on Glacier National Park's west side.

Black Bear
Ursus americanus

There are about 500 black bears in Glacier National Park. Despite their name, black bears can be black, blue-black, cinnamon, brown, blond, and almost white. They evolved in forest environments, and are excellent tree climbers. They are also solitary, wandering territories of 15 to 80 square miles searching for food. Considered opportunistic eaters, their diet includes grasses, roots, nuts, berries, insects, fish, and small mammals. Black bears are extremely adaptable and can develop a preference for human foods and garbage. Bears who become habituated to human food at campgrounds can become aggressive.

When autumn snows arrive, black bears seek a cave, burrow, or tree cavity to make their den. They have also been known to find shelter in crawl spaces under buildings. They pass the winter in a state of dormancy, awakening when disturbed, and may leave their den for brief periods. During the park's long winters, bears live on body fat they stored by gorging all summer and fall. Huckleberries are critical to their health, supplying great amounts of sugar in the fall that turns to fat.

Females give birth to two or three blind, helpless cubs in mid-winter and nurse them in the den until spring. Mother and cubs will stay together for about 2 years. The life expectancy of a black bear in Glacier National Park is up to 20 years.

Best Places to See a Black Bear:

You can see black bears anywhere in both parks. I have encountered more black bears on the St. Mary Falls Trail than any other place. As you drive, check your rearview mirror often. I have seen many black bears running across the road behind my car. You may not see them, but they have likely seen you.

Grizzly Bear

Ursus arctos

"We want to see a bear!" Campground hosts and park rangers hear this exclamation throughout the summer. Some visitors will not consider their vacation complete unless they see a bear. Of course, "a bear" usually means a grizzly, and they want to see it from the safety of their car.

National Park Service.

Bears are wild animals. They are shy, so consider yourself lucky if you see either a black bear or grizzly bear.

Nature has painted the black bear and the grizzly bear with colors that make them hard to tell apart. The 200 to 250 grizzly bears in Glacier

GLACIER'S GRIZZLIES

Grizzly bears can run up to 40 mph. It is a myth that they are unable to run downhill. In truth, they can run as fast downhill as they can uphill. They are also very good swimmers and, despite rumors to the contrary, can climb trees. They have weak eyesight but an excellent sense of smell. Grizzlies evolved on open grasslands where their diet was plants and insects. Today, their diet remains about 70 percent plants. They also eat ground squirrels and winter-killed animals.

National Park can be blond, brown, nearly black, and almost white. Meriwether Lewis called the grizzly bear the "white bear."

Grizzly bears have no natural enemies. They are monarchs of the wilderness. Grizzlies can be unpredictable and may be dangerous if you surprise them, if they think you threaten their cubs, or you get close to their food cache. A grizzly bear may weigh half as much as your car and it can sprint almost twice as fast as an Olympic runner! If you see a grizzly, observe it at a distance that will not change its behavior. Remember, you are a guest in bear country. Be a good one!

Best Places to See a Grizzly Bear:

Glacier and Waterton Lakes national parks are bear country. Expect to see a grizzly bear any time and any place. When hiking, always carry pepper spray. You may see a grizzly along Many Glacier Road from the Apikuni Falls Trailhead to Swiftcurrent Motor Inn, on the south side of Altyn Peak. Early morning and evening hours in late July through September are the best months.

Visiting Bear Country

Bears are big, strong, wild—and therefore, sometimes unpredictable.

Store food in strong odor-tight containers. Enclosed vehicles and campground food lockers offer the best safekeeping; do not leave coolers unattended.

Is it safe to hike in bear country?

Yes. But there are always risks being in bear territory. Read and follow all the suggestions for hiking in bear country provided in the literature you received

David Restivo, National Park Service.

when you entered the park. Look for updated information posted at trailheads. Carry bear pepper spray and read the instructions on its use. Avoid surprising a bear by being alert, hiking mid-day with a group, and making noise when walking. Blind turns, walking into the wind, and being near rushing water require additional caution. Whistle, sing, or clap your hands to alert bears. Never jog on a trail.

What if you see a bear at a distance?
Stay at least 100 yards away. Never stalk a bear.

How do you know if the bear is a grizzly or a black bear?
There is no simple answer. You cannot rely upon color or size to distinguish whether a bear is a grizzly or black. It is more reliable to tell by their noses and shoulders. Black bears have a straight nose; grizzly bears have a dished nose. Grizzly bears have a large hump between their front shoulders; black bears do not. Grizzly hair looks grizzled and shimmery.

ANIMAL GROUPS
Ever think about what units of animals are called? Here is a list of the proper collective nouns:

A gang of moose
A herd of elk
A herd of deer
A sloth of bears
A colony of beavers
A pack of wolves
A knot of toads
A flight of hawks
A hover of trout
A charm of hummingbirds
An army of frogs
An unkindness of ravens
A trip of mountain goats
A flock of bighorn sheep
A dray of squirrels
An earth of foxes
A paddling of ducks (swimming)
A team of ducks (flying)
A murder of crows

What if you encounter a bear at close proximity?
Here are some suggestions from people who have encountered bears:

Grizzly Bear

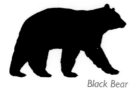
Black Bear

- Look to see if there are cubs nearby. Make sure you are not between a sow and cubs.
- Never run! Instead, back away slowly.
- Avoid looking directly at the bear.
- Talk quietly in a monotone, or not at all.
- Turn sideways, or bend at your knees to appear small.
- Detour around the bear if you must go forward on the trail.

An adult mountain lion weighs between 100 and 250 pounds, and can reach 8 feet in length. They are agile, with the ability to leap up to 20 feet and run up to 35 mph for short distances. The home range of a male may be as much as 265 square miles. Mountain lions are one of the main predators of porcupines in Glacier.

What if the bear advances toward you?

Bears often bluff an assault, then retreat. If a bear is aggressive, use pepper spray. If the bear attacks, protect your chest and abdomen by dropping to the ground on your stomach, or assuming a fetal position. Leave your backpack on and cover the back of your neck with your hands. Do not move until you are certain the bear has left. Report the encounter to a park ranger.

National Park Service.

Mountain Lion

Puma concolor

Cougar, puma, catamount, painter, and panther are all regional names for this big cat. These solitary, secretive, and seldom seen animals are known as mountain lions in Glacier National Park. Common in the park, they usually hide when they sense humans. One of the largest predators in North America, their preferred habitat is wooded areas, where they can sneak up on prey. The big cats are strictly carnivores, with a diet of mule deer, white-tailed deer, and elk. Young, old, and weak prey are the most vulnerable to attack. Mountain lions do not make dens, as such, though they will bed down in caves, rock crevices, and beneath overhangs. They continually move about their home range in search of food. Young are born any time of year. The kittens are blind at birth; their eyes open at two weeks. The young cats may stay with their mother up to two years.

Where You Might See a Mountain Lion:

A chance sighting could occur anywhere in the park. If you do see a mountain lion, it will likely be from your car while the cat is crossing the road. They are easy to identify: with a tail as long as the rest of its body, the animal takes up half the width of the roadway.

BEST PLACES TO SEE WILDLIFE FROM THE ROAD

You want to see wildlife from the road, and in all likelihood, you will. Glacier and Waterton abound with animals you may have seen only in zoos. This landscape is their natural home.

Look for animals along the roadside. Be aware that they sometimes dart in front of cars.

Jason Savage Photography.

Observe the speed limit. Check your rearview mirror often. I have seen several bears cross roads after a car has passed by, its passengers oblivious. When you do see wildlife, don't stop in the roadway. Drive ahead to a pullout.

Here are six areas in the two parks where you are almost guaranteed to see wildlife from the road.

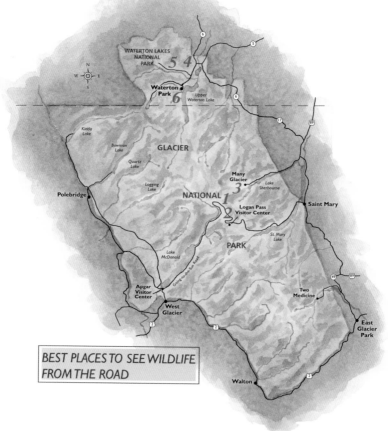

BEST PLACES TO SEE WILDLIFE FROM THE ROAD

1. The Big Bend
Watch for the pullout about 0.25 mile east of the Weeping Wall along Going-to-the-Sun Road. Look for marmots among the rocks and on the hillsides.

2. Going-to-the-Sun Road from 1 mile north of Oberlin Bend to Logan Pass
Bighorn sheep and mountain goats frequent this area throughout summer. You may see them near the road, grazing, or bedded in the meadow near Logan Pass, and navigating the cliffs around Oberlin Falls.

3. Many Glacier Road from the park entrance to the Swiftcurrent Store parking lot
Bears frequent this area during early spring and from late July to mid-September when huckleberries ripen. Watch for bears on the south-facing shoulder of Altyn Peak between Swiftcurrent Falls and the Swiftcurrent Store parking lot.

Bighorn sheep and mountain goats are often seen on the southern slopes of Altyn Peak and in the upper bowl of Mount Henkel any time of day during the height of the visitor season.

4. Bison Paddock Loop Road – Waterton
The only large mammal not found in Glacier National Park but living in Waterton Lakes National Park is the bison. You can see these impressive animals in their prairie habitat by traveling the Paddock Loop Road located 2 miles north of the main park entrance, off Canada Highway 6. Stay in your vehicle.

5. Red Rock Parkway (Waterton) from the junction of Canada Highway 5 to Red Rock Canyon parking area
The parkway follows the Bauerman/Blakiston Creek bottoms. This is prime habitat for grizzly and black bears. There is a reasonable chance that you will see a bear in the early morning and late afternoon.

6. Waterton Townsite
Although wild, the resident mule deer and bighorn sheep that frequent the townsite and adjacent campground are acclimated to people. You will see them walking the streets and laying in grassy areas throughout the townsite.

BEST BIRDS

Montana is home to 294 bird species, and Glacier National Park's diverse habitats provide for more than 260 of them. Several species are iconic representatives of the park—knowing where and when to look for them will increase your chances of enjoying an avian encounter.

Clark's Nutcracker
Nucifraga columbiana

The Clark's nutcracker hides thousands of seeds each year. Unlike your neighborhood squirrel, the bird has a good memory and can remember where to find most of the hidden seeds. Stashing food allows this

Jim Peaco, National Park Service.

year-round resident to begin nesting in late winter. Both the male and female incubate the eggs. Each takes its turn while the other departs to feed at one of their seed caches.

Best Places to See Clark's Nutcrackers:
Clark's nutcrackers are altitudinal migrants. As soon as the young fledge in late spring, the family relocates to subalpine habitats. They migrate back to the valleys in the autumn.

Gray Jay
Perisoreus canadensis

These medium-sized forest denizens glide silently through the conifers, and before you know it, a group has encircled your picnic table or campsite. Also known as "camp robbers," these seemingly affable birds can become a

Jim Peaco, National Park Service.

nuisance as they attempt to steal your food. They are found throughout Glacier and Waterton Lakes national parks year-round. Nesting begins in March, with snow on the ground and temperatures as low as minus 20°F. Females protect the eggs with their thick plumage and a well-insulated nest. They are omnivores that hoard food by using their sticky saliva to glue food bits to tree branches above the height of the eventual snow line.

Best Places to See Gray Jays:
Look for gray jays in campgrounds and picnic areas

Steller's Jay
Cyanocitta stelleri

Accustomed to humans, but naturally wary, the Steller's jay is a cousin of the equally noisy eastern blue jay. Their cries are not limited to scratchy, scolding calls, but include a wide range of vocalizations that mimic sounds

Jim Peaco, National Park Service.

made by birds, squirrels, cats, dogs, chickens, and even mechanical objects. Steller's are sociable, traveling in groups, and you can watch them playing with or chasing each other. A year-round resident, they stash pine seeds for winter food.

Best Places to See Steller's Jays:
Steller's jays live throughout the parks and are often found where there is a closed forest canopy.

Black-capped Chickadee
Poecile atricapillus

Like a sentry, the black-capped chickadee sounds the predator alarm for others in the flock. The more *dee* notes in a *chickadee-dee-dee* call, the higher the threat level. Researchers have found that pygmy owls provoke the most *dees*, as high as 17.

Chickadees spend much of the day picking small insects such as caterpillars off trees. They do not migrate, but flock and travel in large foraging groups.

When food is abundant, they hide seeds and other food, and can remember thousands of hiding places. Every autumn, some of their brain neurons containing old information die and are replaced with new neurons that help them adapt to changes in their social flocks and their environment.

As you walk through forest groves, listen for the high-pitched, two-tone call of the chickadee. Do they see you as a threat? Count the number of *dees* in their call.

Best Places to See Black-capped Chickadees:
You will see chickadees throughout the park in lodgepole pine and Douglas-fir groves.

Western Meadowlark
Sturnella neglecta

Spring and summer are heralded in the parklands by the western meadowlark. You can hear their pure, loud song over a half-mile away. Follow its song and you will see a male perched on a low snag melodiously announcing its territory.

Best Places to See Western Meadowlarks:
Listen for the meadowlark's song around St. Mary, Rising Sun, Cut Bank, the meadows in the North Fork, and the prairie region of Waterton Lakes National Park.

National Park Service.

American Dipper
Cinclus mexicanus

Bird droppings on the boulders in fast moving creeks are a sign that North America's only aquatic songbird is present. Its name comes from its bobbing motion when standing. American dippers build nests on creek bank ledges,

behind waterfalls, and on boulders in rushing water. Their ability to walk and swim underwater to catch insects is fun to watch. They disappear into a creek leaving you to guess where they will emerge. They do not migrate, but may relocate to neighboring lakes in the winter to take advantage of insect hatches.

Best Places to See American Dippers:
Look for dippers near McDonald Creek, and also at Baring Falls, St. Mary Falls, Ptarmigan Falls, Cameron Falls, and along their creeks.

White-tailed Ptarmigan
Lagopus leucurus

Pronounced *TAR-muh-gan*, its scientific name means "hare-footed mountaineer." White as snow in winter but displaying speckled mixed tundra colors in summer, the male white-tailed ptarmigan lives its life in alpine

National Park Service.

regions. Ptarmigans walk with ease on soft, fluffy snow because the extra feathers on the tops and bottoms of their feet act as snowshoes.

Best Places to See White-Tailed Ptarmigans:
Look for white-tailed ptarmigans in the early summer along the Hidden Lake Trail.

Harlequin Duck
Histrionicus histrionicus

Chestnut sides and white patches over a slate gray body identify this summer resident. It is named after the colorfully clad clown character in the whimsical theatrical presentations performed

National Park Service.

throughout Italy in the 16th century. A migratory bird, its autumn commute is to the cliffs above the turbulent coastal waters of Oregon and Washington.

Best Places to See Harlequin Ducks:
Look for harlequin ducks in the McDonald Creek Valley.

Bald Eagle
Haliaeetus leucocephalus

The bald eagle's scientific name signifies a sea *(halo)* eagle *(aeetos)* with a white *(leukos)* head *(cephalus)*. At the time of naming, "bald" meant

TRAVELING COMPANIONS

Chickadees, nuthatches, and brown creepers often travel together. These flocks often attract other species like woodpeckers, kinglets, warblers, and vireos.

The reasons that different species flock together are unclear. Perhaps it is for safety. Each species has a different way of reacting to predators. When the members of one species become frightened, their actions alert other species to potential danger. Another explanation for the flocking behavior is that the diets of the birds are similar. One species may "inform" the others of a food source. Nuthatches and brown creepers illustrate this. Both species feed on the same food—insects concealed around the edges of tree bark. Yet they do not compete; the nuthatch works down the tree trunk feeding on insects at the top edges of the bark, while the brown creeper spirals up the tree trunk extracting the same insect species from under the bottom crevices of the bark.

Small songbirds migrating through Glacier National Park often join these groups. Watch for these flocks during the spring and autumn—they can alert you to the presence of interesting migrant birds.

"white," not hairless. The official designation of the bald eagle as the emblem of the United States came in 1787 because of "its long life, great strength, and majestic looks," and also because it was believed to exist only on this continent. A robust debate preceded the designation, as political leaders, including Benjamin Franklin, disapproved, stating that the bald eagle was of "bad moral character," proposing, instead, the turkey as the national bird.

National Park Service.

Best Places to See Bald Eagles:

Glacier National Park supports many pairs of eagles during the summer. Bald eagles mostly eat fish. Look for them around lakes, especially in the North Fork.

Osprey
Pandion haliaetus

Once called fish hawks, osprey are sometimes confused for bald eagles. A spectacular sight is an osprey carrying a fish head-first in its talons. You might witness a bald eagle harassing an osprey in aerial combat to get it to release the fish. If successful, the eagle will dive to capture the fish before it reaches the ground.

SNAGS: WILDLIFE SKYSCRAPERS

Look for standing dead trees as you walk the trails and drive the roads. The numerous avalanche chutes you can see from pullouts along Going-to-the-Sun Road between Packers Roost and the Wild Goose Island overlook are good places to look. Known as "snags" (an old Scandinavian word for "stump of a tree"), these dead trees are critical to the ecology.

Snags are home to insects, provide nesting for birds and squirrels, and extend shelter to a myriad of animals during storms. The tallest snags provide the best animal shelter. These "skyscraper" environments limit predator access to roosting and nesting wildlife. Here is a list of ways that snags help wildlife:

- *Eagles, herons, osprey, and hawks perch and nest on the tops of snags*
- *Woodpeckers and brown thrashers feed on insects*
- *Bats roost and birds nest under overhanging loose bark*
- *Woodpeckers, nuthatches, wood ducks, owls, pine martens, and squirrels nest in snag cavities*

Nationwide, 85 percent of all bird species use snags for nesting, shelter, or food. Nutrients bound in snags begin recycling when wind, rain, or an avalanche sends them crashing to the ground. Snags that fall into creeks, marshes, and lakes help create spawning areas for fish and habitat for aquatic insects that then become food for fish. Look around you ... how many wildlife skyscrapers do you see?

Best Places to See Osprey:

The best place to see an osprey is at the St. Mary Visitor Center, where the National Park Service has provided a nearby nesting site and a spotting scope to view the nest. Also watch for osprey perched in trees or in flight above lakes and streams.

National Park Service.

IMPORTANT INSECTS

When you think of Glacier National Park's iconic animals, insects probably don't spring to mind. Although you might view some of them as nuisances, they play vital roles in the park's ecology. Insects pollinate most of the park's flowers, trees, and shrubs, and are an integral part

USDA Forest Service.

of forest succession through infestation. They are also food for many animal species.

During late summer, grizzly bears spend much of their time in the rocky subalpine meadows and alpine tundra. The bears go there to escape the heat, to locate rocks with salt-rich minerals, and to find high-nutrition army cutworm moths and ladybug beetles.

Army cutworm moths surface from the soil of the prairies in late June. Soon after, they fly to the mountain peaks to escape the summer heat. At night, they feed on flowers; during the day, they hide under small rocks. Grizzly bears know to return each summer to these alpine areas, and that the moths are more nutritious than large prey. Plus, they are easier to catch! Lying on their bellies and scooping with their paws, grizzly bears can eat as many as 40,000 moths per day. Researchers found that each moth provides about half a calorie of nutrition, so on a good day, a bear can add 20,000 calories to his store of fat! Look for overturned rocks and logs—a bear may have had a feast!

Ladybug beetles also arise from the eastern prairies and migrate to the mountain peaks. In September, some rocks are so thickly covered in ladybugs that grizzly bears lick them up by the mouthful. Beetles that escape this bruin raid crawl under the rocks and go into hibernation until June. The deep snows of the high country provide insulation against extreme cold. Prairie winters do not provide enough snow insulation for the ladybugs to survive the frigid temperatures. The ladybugs migrate down to the prairies by June.

Mosquitoes abound in Glacier and Waterton during the warm months. You'll find swarms of them in cool, damp areas as well as warm, sunny hillsides. What are they good for? Mosquitoes are important because they pollinate plants. Only female mosquitoes bite people. They seek the protein in blood needed for their eggs to develop properly. Female mosquitoes are attracted to carbon dioxide. They can sense the carbon dioxide you exhale. Long sleeves, pants, and socks, as well as a bandanna tied around your neck that has been sprayed with a repellent—these are the most effective ways to keep mosquitoes from biting. If you do get a mosquito bite, even with all your precautions, just consider it a souvenir from the park.

The mountain pine beetle can be found throughout both parks, especially in low-lying areas where lodgepole pine forests grow. Pine beetles burrow under the bark, lay eggs, and the larvae eat their way around the tree, cutting off the flow of nutrients. Beetles and their larvae are nutritious to woodpeckers that eat them in great numbers. Trees ooze sap in defense against the boring beetles, but many trees soon die after infestation. Pine beetles have killed thousands of the park's trees, making them tinder for fires. Fire kills the beetles, the forest regenerates, and the cycle continues.

Photo by Bruce Dellard.

BEST WILDFLOWERS

Labor Day visitors are often surprised to see magnificent wildflower displays at Logan Pass. Why are there so many flowers this late in summer? It makes sense if you think of Glacier National Park as a "vertical garden."

Photo by Sam Simpson.

Generally, every 100 feet gain in elevation delays blooming by about one day. So springtime flowers that bloom on the McDonald Creek valley floor in May will not open at Logan Pass until July. Likewise, flowers opening in late July on the valley floor will blossom a month later atop the pass.

Why is there such a variety of glorious wildflower displays park-wide? This is because species unique to the plains, Pacific Coast, Rocky Mountains, and alpine tundra meet here at the Crown of the Continent in an ecosystem found nowhere else.

Most of the flowering plants are perennial. Their roots remain alive but dormant over the winter, so plants are ready to grow and blossom soon after snowmelt. Thousands of generations of adaptations have made them precisely acclimated to their habitat. Some have been alive for more than 100 years. Undisturbed in this wilderness, they have become the ideal of their species.

The National Park Service estimates that more than 1,000 different plant species live in Glacier National Park. Forty-one species are deemed rare in Montana and 28 are found nowhere else in the state. Wildflowers that are most associated with the park are beargrass, glacier lily, fireweed, prickly rose, paintbrush, silky lupine, harebell, and sticky geranium.

Beargrass
Xerophyllum tenax

It is a myth that bears rely on this lily to satisfy their diet. If you see beargrass' tall stalks with missing flower heads, know that other animals, including rodents, elk, and bighorn sheep, nibbled here.

Photo by Linda Duvanich.

You will find complete hillsides covered in beargrass blooms during some summers. Individual plants bloom every 3 to 10 years; if you are fortunate, you will see a whole population of beargrass blooming together. It's a beautiful sight!

Where You Can Find Beargrass:
Beargrass grows throughout the park. You can find a half-acre field north of Going-to-the-Sun Road at Logan Pass.

Fireweed
Epilobium angustifolium

Fireweed is a fast-growing pioneer perennial that colonizes disturbed areas by spreading roots and seeds. Like dandelion seeds, fireweed seeds can travel by wind a considerable distance. A northern hemisphere native, it became known as *bombweed* in Europe due to its rapid colonization of bomb craters in World War II. It establishes in burnt areas, clear-cut forests, and along roadsides, and adds nutrients to the soil essential for plant succession. Some people make jellies and syrups from the blossoms. Fireweed is browsed by deer, elk, and grizzly bears.

Where You Can Find Fireweed:
You will see fireweed along all of the roads, in avalanche chutes, and in recently burned areas.

Glacier Lily
Erythronium grandiflorum

Glacier lily is the most emblematic flower in the park. They emerge along the edges of melting snowfields and within 10 weeks complete their recurrent growth cycle.

The underground bulb or "corm" is a favorite food of rodents and grizzlies. Grizzly bear claws are specialized for digging. Often the bears dig up whole fields of glacier lilies. Some people say that the corms taste like green beans. Deer, elk, bighorn sheep, and mountain goats eat the seedpods.

Where You Can Find Glacier Lilies:
Logan Pass is famous for its carpet of glacier lilies. You will also find them scattered throughout moist areas.

Harebell
Campanula rotundifolia

This delicate-looking flower is quite hardy and found throughout Glacier and Waterton national parks. It is adapted to a variety of habitats and can be found in full sun or shade, dry or moist soils, and in forests, meadows, cliffs, lake beaches, as well as roadside gravel. Harebells are found at the park's lowest elevations in the Belly River drainage and on mountainsides up to 11,000 feet.

According to European folklore, harebells grew in places that hares lived, or that witches used its flower juices to change themselves into hares. Hence its common name.

Where You Can Find Harebell:
Everywhere. At lower elevations, look for blue bells atop tall (12- to 15-inch) stems. On high mountain slopes, blossoms often trail from short runners close to the ground.

Paintbrush
Castilleja spp.

This showy perennial is named for its colorful ragged bracts that appear to have been dipped in paint. The colorful bracts stay vivid longer than the petals of flowering plants, which lose their color as the flowers wilt. Paintbrush's true flowers, tiny and yellow, are hidden within the bracts. Several species of paintbrush are found in the parks. Hummingbirds seek its nectar. Many botanists believe that paintbrush plants and hummingbirds co-evolved. Don't look for paintbrush in your local nursery. It does not domesticate.

Where You Can Find Paintbrush:
Paintbrush is common along Going-to-the-Sun Road, Two Medicine Road, Many Glacier Road, Red Rock Parkway and Akamina Parkway in Waterton, and many lower-elevation trails.

Prickly Rose (aka Wild Rose)
Rosa acicularis

Prickly rose has attractive pink blooms, thorns, and large red fruit (hips) that persist in winter. This species' weaker, numerous "prickles" distinguish it from prairie rose *(R. woodsii)* which has heavier thorns. Some people make jelly or wine from the outer husk of the rose hips, which are

Photo by Sam Simpson.

rich in vitamins. The seeds within are unpalatable and can irritate the digestive tract. Prickly rose blooms in early summer. Also watch for the blossom on Alberta license plates.

Where You Can Find Prickly Rose:
Look for rose blossoms in woods and open places throughout the park, especially near Rising Sun, next to the Many Glacier Road, and along the Red Rock Parkway in Waterton.

Silky Lupine
Lupinus sericeus

This ubiquitous perennial was blamed for a crime it did not commit.

Botanists accused it of devouring soil nutrients and gave it the name *Lupinus,* Latin for wolf. Further research acquitted it, showing that lupine plants preferred poor soil, rather than made it. The plant works with mycorrhizal fungi to create the soil nutrients it needs. Columbian ground squirrels eat the leaves and flowers. Bighorn sheep feed on dead leaves and stems in the winter.

Where You Can Find Lupine:

Look for the blue, purple, pink, and (rarer) white flowers in June and July along road cuts and in rocky, open meadows.

Sticky Geranium

Geranium viscosissimum

Sticky hairs cover the stems and lower leaves of this geranium. Avoid handling the plant or you will need to scrub the gumminess off your hands. The gluey substance has enzymes found in carnivorous plants, leading some botanists to think that sticky geranium is evolving in that direction. Deer, elk, and moose eat the young leaves and the flowers, which are pink, but can be white or lavender.

Where You Can Find Sticky Geranium:

Common throughout Glacier and Waterton, you will see sticky geranium in open grasslands, along roadsides, and lining trails.

Best Places to See Wildflowers

Most first-time visitors to Glacier National Park tour the Going-to-the-Sun Road and the Many Glacier area. Expecting only to savor geologic wonders, many are thunderstruck by the profusion and variety of wildflowers along the roads and in meadows. Here are some of the best places with easy access by car or foot to relish the park's impressive floral displays. Make sure your camera is ready!

Best Wildflower Meadows:

Early Season (May, June, and July)
- Two Dog Flats
- Rising Sun

BEST PLACES TO SEE WILDFLOWERS

- Cut Bank Creek area
- Many Glacier Road near Apikuni Falls Trailhead
- Paradise Point (Two Medicine)
- Hidden Meadow (North Fork)
- Big Prairie (North Fork)
- Grinnell Glacier Trail

Mid Season (July and August)

- Logan Pass
- The Garden Wall (Highline Trail)
- Iceberg Lake Trail
- Big Bend, Going-to-the-Sun Road
- Siyeh Creek at Siyeh Bend, Going-to-the-Sun Road
- Oberlin Bend, Going-to-the-Sun Road

- Southeast flank of Piegan Mountain, south of Siyeh Bend, Going-to-the-Sun Road
- South flank of Altyn Peak north of Many Glacier Road
- Running Eagle Falls Trail, Two Medicine Road
- Grinnell Glacier Trail, Many Glacier Area

Late Season (August and September)
- Hidden Lake Overlook at Logan Pass
- The Garden Wall (Highline Trail)
- Iceberg Lake Trail

Wildflowers in Waterton

Of all the species of wildflowers that occur in Alberta, more than half are found in Waterton Lakes National Park, which boasts more than 1,000 species of vascular plants within its 195 square miles. The most easily accessed wildflower displays in Waterton include the following.

The main entrance road (Highway 5) and Bison Paddock (on Highway 6 north of the entrance station) provide views of early season prairie and foothills flowers such as coneflowers, asters, prairie smoke, and Canada anemone.

Along the Red Rock Parkway, pause at Crandell Mountain Campground and Blakiston Creek meadows along the last 2 miles of road to see fields of lupine, mint, Jacob's ladder, fleabane, and geranium.

Drive to Cameron Lake at the end of the Akamina Parkway to see mountain slopes decked in arrowleaf balsamroot, lupine, and—in some years—beargrass.

Even a short hike along any of Waterton's many forested, streamside trails will reveal paintbrush, monkeyflowers, orchids, scorpionweed, and columbine. You'll have to hike to higher elevations to see shooting stars, glacier lilies, and cinquefoil.

BEST HUCKLEBERRIES

National Park Service.

Huckleberries
Vaccinium globulare

Huckleberries are more than candy on a stem for black bears and grizzly bears. They mean survival, as the bears crave them to build fat before hibernation. Huckleberries provide up to one third of a bear's nourishment during late summer. Pregnant bears will lose cubs over winter if they do not get enough berry nourishment.

Montanans' love of huckleberries has elevated the berries to cult status. Look for huckleberry celebrations during August. Nearby, retail shops sell aromatic soaps, lotions, and huckleberry-flavored lip balms, while restaurants serve ice cream, pastries, milkshakes, and pies. Try them all, and see if you agree with the bears and the locals that huckleberries are fantastic.

Where You Can Find Huckleberries:

You will find huckleberry bushes along most sunny trails in Glacier National Park. They can also be found throughout Many Glacier Valley, where bears gorge themselves on huckleberries from August to mid-September. Trails are often closed for bears when berries are ripe. Bears get first pick.

BEST TREES

Glacier National Park sits at an ecological crossroads where the Pacific Northwest meets the Great Plains and north meets south. Prevailing weather systems from the Pacific and the Arctic bump into the north-south mountain ranges and create vastly different conditions over short distances. Elevational differences within the park, from valley bottoms to alpine summits, also shape life here. Scientists have identified five major "life zones" within the park based on the plant communities that thrive in each. Three zones—aspen parkland, montane, and subalpine—are defined by the forests that grow in them. The other two

David Restivo, National Park Service.

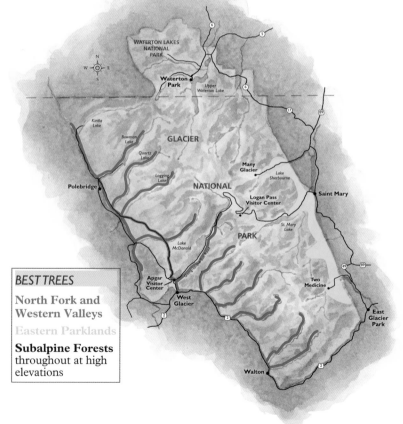

BEST TREES

North Fork and Western Valleys

Eastern Parklands

Subalpine Forests throughout at high elevations

zones—grasslands and alpine tundra—are home to few if any tree species. Indicator tree species may dominate a zone, but in the park they are often found in other zones as well.

Western Valleys

Moist Pacific air collides with the mountain peaks, bringing rain and snow to the western slopes. The valleys

National Park Service.

are characterized by groves of western redcedar and western hemlock. The Trail of the Cedars near Avalanche Campground is an excellent place to see the redcedars and hemlock trees that make up this wet forest environment. Little direct sunlight reaches the ground in cedar-hemlock groves, making them cool with thick undergrowth that thrives in shade. Fires are less common, and some trees are 500 years old. Other trees that dominate the western slopes are western larch, Engelmann spruce, Douglas-fir, and lodgepole pine.

Several species of bats, northern flying squirrels, pine martens, and black bears live in the western valleys. Most of these animals are nocturnal.

Western Redcedar

Thuja plicata

Western redcedar trees in Glacier National Park grow best in moist, streamside soils where they have shallow root systems. A walk through the Trail of the Cedars will take you to a picturesque example of an upended exposed root system of a western redcedar.

Western Hemlock

Tsuga heterophylla

The western hemlock is a shade-tolerant tree that has dense branching close to the ground. It is the lower growing tree you will find in the Trail of the Cedars, and in Douglas-fir stands. Hemlock was named after a European weed that has a similar smell.

Douglas-fir
Pseudotsuga menziesii

Douglas-fir trees are central to wildlife needs in Glacier National Park. The profuseness of Douglas-fir cones provide a feast for red squirrels, chipmunks, and countless insects that feed on the seeds before the cones open. A Blackfeet Indian story tells of mice that hid in Douglas-fir cones to avoid the pre-human spirit, Naapi. You can identify Douglas-fir cones by the 3-tooth bracts extending past the cone's scales; can you see the tails and hind legs of mice in the shape of the bracts?

David Restivo, National Park Service.

Eastern Parklands

The open spaces in eastern Glacier National Park are called parklands. Large groves of quaking aspen define the parklands and are found in the St. Mary, Many Glacier, Belly River, and Two Medicine areas. Visit St. Mary campground and stand among the trees. The slightest breeze will tell you why they are called quaking aspens.

Quaking aspens are deciduous trees, losing their leaves each autumn but only after they turn a brilliant yellow. During autumn, the groves paint the parklands with liquid sunshine.

Animals you might see in the parklands are moose, elk, deer, grizzly bears, black bears, coyotes, and wolves. Look for hawks and American kestrel hunting over the open spaces.

Quaking Aspen
Populus tremuloides

The quaking aspen is the most widely distributed tree species in North America. Most of their seeds are sterile, but their light weight allows them to be broadcast by wind over great distances. The viable seeds germinate with ease along stream banks where they serve as soil stabilizers, and in disturbed areas where they become pioneer species. Once established, they can propagate by their roots, forming large dome-shaped groves with the older trees in the center. These genetically identical tree islands are apparent in the Many Glacier area and St. Mary.

North Fork Valley

This zone is a broad flood plain of the North Fork of the Flathead River. It includes river bottom and the shoulder of the Livingston Range. It contains a wide variety of tree species; the dominant species are ponderosa pine, lodgepole pine, and western larch.

Animals you might see in the

David Restivo, National Park Service.

North Fork Valley are moose, elk, deer, mountain lions, black bears, grizzly bears, coyotes, and wolves.

Lodgepole Pine
Pinus contorta

This tree gets its name from the fact that native people traditionally used the trunk of this tree to make the frames of their tepees (lodges). The tree is also frequently used to build the shells of log homes. The scientific name of this species does not describe the straight and long appearance of these trees. The botanists who first identified the characteristics of the lodgepole pine were studying specimens growing on the north Pacific Coast. There, the lodgepole's growth pattern is affected by salt air and wind, causing the tree to grow twisted and stunted, hence the scientific name, *Pinus contorta* (contorted pine).

Ponderosa Pine
Pinus ponderosa

The ponderosa pine is recognized by its jigsaw puzzle-like bark. Take the opportunity to smell the bark of a large pine. The tree might be giving off an odor. What fragrance do you detect? (Some say ponderosas carry the scent of vanilla, others say butterscotch.)

The ponderosa pine is the state tree of Montana. Older ponderosas are sometimes called yellowbellies because of the color of their trunk.

Fire benefits ponderosa pine communities by removing plants and trees that compete for water and nutrients in the soil.

Western Larch
Larix occidentalis

Western larch is one of only three tree species world-wide that is both coniferous and deciduous. Its needles turn bright yellow, then golden in October. It is a spectacular sight to see the golden larch trees mixed with dark green ponderosa pines and lodgepole pines. By December, all of the needles have fallen. Only two other species on Earth are both deciduous and coniferous: bald cypress and the dawn redwood.

Subalpine Forests

Trees of the subalpine forests characterize the upper reaches of Glacier National Park: subalpine fir, Engelmann spruce, and white-bark pine. Living near timberline are subalpine firs and Engelmann spruce trees. A walk around the Logan Pass Visitor Center will introduce you to these trees, which appear miniature because of the assault of constant wind and winter ice. Shrubby forms of subalpine fir trees bunched together are known as krummholz. You can "feel" the park's extreme weather by just seeing an island of these stunted trees.

Look for Columbian ground squirrels, hoary marmots, bighorn sheep, mountain goats, pikas, and chipmunks in the forests of the subalpine zone.

Subalpine Fir
Abies lasiocarpa

A popular Christmas tree, subalpine firs are forest pioneers on disturbed sites. New trees assist in rehabilitating the landscape by protecting watersheds and providing cover for wildlife. Near tree-line, subalpine firs can withstand Glacier National Park's coldest temperatures. Heavy snow loads press trunks and lower branches to the ground where they root and perpetuate the krummholz growth pattern.

Engelmann Spruce
Picea engelmannii

The trees that you see at timberline include Engelmann spruce. They survive in the highest and coldest areas of the park, tolerating minus 50°F. Lower-elevation trees can grow to 150 feet tall over the span of 400 years. The fine-lined, lightweight, and straight wood grain is perfect for piano sound boards.

Whitebark Pine
Pinus albicaulis

The whitebark pine species co-evolved with the Clark's nutcracker, which eats or caches the seeds. Seeds not retrieved from caches may germinate and become established seedlings. Red squirrels harvest the cones and store them in middens on the forest floor. Black and grizzly bears raid these for the energy-rich seeds, making whitebark pine a keystone species of the subalpine forests.

KRUMMHOLZ FORMATIONS AND FLAG TREES

Krummholz (German for "crooked wood") is a phenomenon of subalpine forests. Exposure to wind and cold causes trees to become stunted and twisted. They survive where they are sheltered by rock formations, protected under snow, or grow in a tight group. The protected areas of these trees continue to grow, causing them to become characteristically compact.

A variation on krummholz is a flag tree. Branches on the windward side are killed or deformed by icy winds that destroy new growth, giving the tree a characteristic flag-like appearance. The lower portion of the tree is often protected by snow and lacks the flagging. Whereas krummholz grow in small groups, flag trees often grow alone. In Glacier National Park, the species that form krummholz include subalpine fir, Engelmann spruce, and limber pine. Logan Pass Visitor Center is a good place to see krummholz.

BEST NAMES OF NATURAL FEATURES

A host of expressive, interesting names have been given to various park features. Many names are from the Blackfeet Nation, some from the Kootenai People, and a few were given by Euro-Americans. The following are the Best Names of Natural Features you will likely see during your visit.

Bird Woman Falls
The falls could be named for *Sacajawea*, the young Shoshone mother who helped guide Lewis and Clark on their historic journey through the Northwest from 1804 to 1806. Her Hidatsa name translates as "Bird Woman."

Going-to-the-Sun
James Willard Schultz likely named the mountain. Why he selected the name is uncertain. Schultz was a white man who lived among the Blackfeet in the late 1800s. The road was given the same name upon its completion in 1933.

Running Eagle Falls
The feature is named for the place where a Blackfeet woman warrior (Pitamahkan or Running Eagle) came to seek her vision.

Sacred Dancing
The area around Lake McDonald was referred to long ago as "a good place to dance" by the Kootenai People. Euro-Americans applied the name to the lake and the cascade on McDonald Creek.

Wild Goose Island
Named for the Canada geese that nest here.

You will need to hike to get close to the colorfully named mountains, waterfalls, lakes, and glaciers listed below.

Mountains

- Dusty Star (from the Blackfeet *iszíká-kakátósi*, meaning "smoking star" or comet), Eagle Plume (named for *Pitái-sapop*, a Kaina chief)

- Dancing Lady

- Almost a Dog (named for a Blackfeet warrior, *Imazi-imita*)

- Angel Wing

- Bearhat (named by James Schultz in honor of *Klawla kayuka*, a Kootenai chief)

- Brave Dog (named for the *Mázix*, a group in the All Comrades Societies, a social order of the Blackfeet)

- Crowfeet (named after a 19th century Kaina chief)

- Curly Bear (named for *Kyáiyo-xusi*, a Blackfeet warrior and historian, who worked with James Schultz to provide place names within Glacier)

- Mad Wolf (named for *Sáiyi*, a Piegan elder famed for recovering a sacred albino otter hide bowcase from the Assiniboine; Mount Siyeh is also named after him)

- Rising Wolf (in Blackfeet, *Mahkúyi-opuáhsin*, the name given to Hugh Monroe, a Canadian trapper who married *Sinopáki*, daughter of Bird Woman and Lone Walker, a Piegan leader; Monroe lived from 1799 to 1892)

- Running Rabbit (named for a Kaina chief, *Aazist-omahkan*)

Waterfalls

- Dawn Mist (a fictitious heroine in the novel *The White Quiver* (1913), popularized in Great Northern Railway advertising)

- Beaver Medicine
- Golden Stairs
- Morning Eagle (named for *Apinákui-Pita*, Blackfeet medicine man)
- White Quiver (a Piegan man famed for once rustling horses from the Royal Canadian Mounted Police)
- Feather Plume

Lakes

- Buffalo Woman (name of a Blackfeet woman; in 1929 the lake was named in her honor by H. A. Noble, general manager of the Glacier Park Hotel Company)
- Cobalt
- Falling Leaf
- Moran's Bathtub (possibly named after miners Tom and Pat Moran; shown on today's maps as Swiftcurrent Ridge Lake)
- Morning Star
- Snow Moon
- Medicine Grizzly
- Iceberg
- Crypt (Waterton)

Glaciers

- Pumpelly (named for Raphel Pumpelly, (1837-1923), a prominent geologist)
- Salamander
- Blackfoot
- Thunderbird
- Vulture
- Weasel Collar (an old Kootenai tribal name)

BEST ACTIVITIES FOR CHILDREN

Writing in *The Sense of Wonder,* Rachel Carson observed, *"If a child is to keep alive his inborn sense of wonder . . . he needs the companionship of at least one adult who can share it, discovering with him the joy, excitement, and mystery of the world we live in. "* Glacier National Park is more than exceptional scenery. It is like no other place on Earth. Its broad range of natural resources and its cultural heritage can inspire a kinship that provokes the lasting pleasures of contact with the natural world. The park is not for adults alone. Here is a list of activities you can do with your children to increase their awareness of Glacier National Park's wonders.

David Restivo, National Park Service.

Explore, Learn, and Protect as a Junior Ranger
Glacier National Park's Junior Ranger Program is designed to allow children to explore the park at their own pace. Kids attend a ranger-led program and complete at least five activities in a Junior Ranger booklet. Junior Ranger badges are awarded to a child when a park ranger checks the youngster's finished booklet. Booklets are available at visitor centers in Apgar, Logan Pass, and St. Mary.

Learn About the Local Culture
American Indians have revered the landscape of Glacier National Park for untold generations. The park remains a rich stronghold of tribal heritage. Each summer, local visual and performing artists share their culture with park visitors. Blackfeet singers, dancers, and storytellers reveal their deep traditional connection with the park at campfire programs. Look for presentations at St. Mary, Logan Pass, Many Glacier, Two Medicine, Lake McDonald, Rising Sun, and Apgar Village.

Skip Rocks
Gentle wave action for thousands of years has smoothed rocks into perfectly flat silver dollar-size skipping stones at several of the lakes. Look

for abundant stones along the shoreline of Lake McDonald between Apgar Village and the North Shore Ranger Station. On calm days, McDonald's glassy waters make it an ideal lake for rock skipping.

Ride a Bicycle

There are two designated bicycle paths in Glacier National Park, both in the Apgar area. The Fish Creek Bike Path is a 1.2-mile trail. Connect with the path at the Fish Creek Campground or at the first right past the McDonald Creek Bridge along the Camas Road in Apgar. The McDonald Creek Bike Path is a 1.5-mile trail between Apgar and the west park entrance. You will find the path 50 yards south of the Apgar Visitor Center. Both trails are paved, leisurely, and have little elevation change.

Fish at McDonald Creek

At lower McDonald Creek, west of Apgar Village, you will discover a "fishing for fun" catch-and-release area. Easy to access, you and your child can try your luck at landing cutthroat trout, whitefish, rainbow trout, and brook trout. Make sure that you obtain the current fishing regulations, available at any ranger station or visitor center.

Attend an Evening Program

Relax, and learn about the diversity of Glacier National Park with the help of an experienced park ranger. Topics include bears, birds, history, climate change, and glaciers. Review the park newspaper and select a campground amphitheater presentation at Rising Sun, Apgar, Fish Creek, Many Glacier, Two Medicine, or an auditorium program at the St. Mary Visitor Center, Lake McDonald Lodge, or at the Lucerne Room of the Many Glacier Hotel. All programs are less than one hour.

Go on a Ranger-led Tour

The National Park Service also offers a variety of ranger-led walks. Most are more than two hours, some as many as eight. The wildflower walk at Many Glacier and the Oxbow Stroll at Lake McDonald are about one hour. Consider combining two modes of transportation with the St. Mary Lake Boat Trip and Hike. This 3.5-hour experience from Rising Sun combines a cruise on the lake to a boat dock where you disembark for a 3-mile round-trip hike to St. Mary Falls. Catch a later boat for your return.

Take a Walk in the Park

Do you want to explore the park with your child without a guide? Glacier National Park has 151 trails totaling over 750 miles. You would need several summers to experience the entire park by foot. Start with short, educational, and exciting walks that will inspire your child to want to return for more challenging experiences. Enhance your hike by checking out one of the Glacier Park Family Backpacks at the St. Mary or Apgar visitor centers.

Nature Trails

- Self–guided brochures for these nature trails are provided at the trailheads and available at the visitor centers. See pages 19–26 for details.

- Trail of the Cedars, 1.0-mile loop from Going-to-the-Sun Road, just north of Avalanche Creek Campground.

- Swiftcurrent Lake Nature Trail, 2.6-mile loop from the shoreline of Swiftcurrent Lake at the south end of Many Glacier Hotel.

- Running Eagle Falls, 0.3 mile round-trip, the trailhead is 1 mile west of the Two Medicine entrance station on U.S. Highway 89.

Short Hikes

- Avalanche Lake, 4.2 miles round-trip. The trail starts just north of Avalanche Creek Campground.

- Hidden Lake Overlook, 3 miles round-trip. The trailhead is behind the Logan Pass Visitor Center.

- St. Mary Falls and Virginia Falls, 3.6 miles round-trip. The trailhead is 10.5 miles west of St. Mary on Going-to-the-Sun Road, marked with a sign.

- Beaver Pond Loop, 3-mile loop from the 1913 Ranger Station in St. Mary.

- Redrock Falls, 5 miles round-trip. The trailhead is at the western end of the Swiftcurrent Store parking lot in Many Glacier. Follow the Swiftcurrent Pass Trail.

Visit the Discovery Cabin in Apgar Village

The Discovery Cabin in Apgar Village has antlers, horns, rocks, pine cones, animal skins, and skulls of native animals for children to investigate. Exhibits educate about the park's biological diversity. Discovery Cabin interpreters offer demonstrations, workshops, and programs about the animals and habitats that will enrich your child's experience of the park.

Read Aloud

Be prepared. A rainy day or a lull in activities gives you an opportunity to read a book with your child. Many entertaining and informative books are available at the Glacier Natural History Association bookstore in West Glacier and at retailers throughout the park. Pick some that you want to read and that will give your child a better understanding of Glacier National Park's heritage. Here are a few of the books that are available:

- *Black Bear Babies*
- *Grizzly Babies*
- *Moose Babies*
- *Glacier Babies*
- *Mountain Goat Babies*
- *Go Wild for Puzzles: Glacier National Park*, Robert Rath
- *Who Pooped in the Park? Glacier National Park*, Gary Robson
- *Going to Glacier*, Alan Leftridge
- *Bird Feats of Montana*, Deborah Richie Oberbillig
- *Bug Feats of Montana*, Deborah Richie Oberbillig

Take a Boat Tour

Concessionaires operate tour boats on St. Mary Lake, Two Medicine Lake, Lake McDonald, Swiftcurrent Lake, and Lake Josephine. Two Medicine Lake, Swiftcurrent Lake, and Lake Josephine are 30-minute excursions. All three take you to the end of the lake where you can elect to return by boat or hike back. Lake McDonald and St. Mary Lake boat trips are 90 minutes long.

Go for a Paddle

You can rent kayaks, canoes, and rowboats with all the necessary gear, including life vests, at Two Medicine Lake, Lake McDonald, Swiftcurrent Lake, and Cameron Lake in Waterton Lakes National Park. Go in the morning when the water is calm, before afternoon winds stir up waves.

Ride a River Raft

Several rafting companies outside the park offer half-day and full-day trips on the Middle Fork of the Flathead River. Expect to see wildlife. A favorite half-day stretch of whitewater is from the Moccasin Creek put-in (mile marker 159 on U.S. Highway 2) to West Glacier.

Ride a Horse

Get a sense of what it must have been like to see Glacier National Park before the opening of Going-to-the-Sun Road. Outfitters offer horseback rides from West Glacier, the Lake McDonald Lodge area, and Many Glacier Hotel.

Reflect

Today's fast-paced, gadget-filled lifestyle is busy with distractions. Glacier National Park presents wonderful opportunities to take a deep breath and reconnect with the natural world. Find a quiet, peaceful spot. Challenge your child to sit in solitude for 5 or 10 minutes. (Try it yourself, too!) Ask them to think about what they hear, smell, and see. Encourage them to write or draw about the experience and what their senses revealed to them. As they settle in for the night, ask your child to reflect on what they liked about the day's activities.

View the Night Sky

The U.S. Census Bureau estimates that 82 percent of Americans live in cities and suburbs. Living under the glow of urban lights, children do not experience the excitement of seeing the Milky Way, August's Perseid meteor shower, or summer constellations. Glacier National Park's dark nighttime skies allow you to stargaze with your child. Do it on your own, or inquire at the St. Mary Visitor Center to learn if a star-watch program is scheduled during your stay.

Visit the Alberta Visitor Center in West Glacier

See a *T-rex* skeleton and go on a simulated bobsled ride. The visitor center includes hands-on discovery tables and displays about area history.

Why is there an Alberta Visitor Center in West Glacier? Because Glacier National Park partnered with Waterton Lakes National Park in Alberta to be the world's first International Peace Park, established in 1937. Together, they share management goals that protect the natural and cultural heritage of the "Crown of the Continent."

BEST PLACES TO WATCH SUNRISE AND SUNSET

David Restivo, National Park Service.

    Sunrise and sunset bathe Waterton-Glacier International Peace Park's peaks and lakes in dramatic light, enjoyable from almost anywhere in the parks. The following easy-to-get-to locations are particularly photogenic and romantic at dawn and day's end.

Sunrise

- Apgar Village, shore of Lake McDonald
- Sun Point
- Bowman Lake Campground
- Chief Mountain viewpoint
- Granite Park Chalet
- Prince of Wales Hotel, Waterton

Sunset

- Sundeck of the Many Glacier Hotel
- Vista windows of the Many Glacier Hotel
- Boat dock at the Lake McDonald Lodge
- St. Mary Visitor Center
- Wild Goose Island pullout
- Sun Point
- Granite Park Chalet
- Prince of Wales Hotel, Waterton

BEST HONEYMOON SUITE

Some newlyweds opt for the adventure of backpacking into Glacier National Park's wilderness to celebrate their marriage. Others are interested in a romantic lodge experience. For the latter, Glacier Park Lodge is the best bet.

The "Big Tree Lodge," as the Blackfeet people dubbed it upon its completion in 1913, offers several types of rooms, including a main lodge suite and a deluxe room in the Great Northern Wing. The rooms are spacious, with traditional Western adornments, and quiet, without the distractions of Internet service and televisions.

The Lodge is self-contained, with a large dining room, a bar, a gift shop, a variety of Red Bus Tour options into the park, an outdoor swimming pool, a nine-hole golf course, a nine-hole pitch 'n' putt course, and a day spa featuring massages.

BEST THINGS TO DO ON A RAINY (OR SNOWY) DAY

David Restivo, National Park Service.

The one constant of mountain weather is how quickly it can change. In Glacier National Park, a warm, sunny summer day can suddenly turn to cold rain and even snow. The peaks wring precipitation from moist Pacific air masses, and Arctic air sliding down from Canada can bring snow anytime. (In August 2005, an 8-inch snowfall sent many surprised hikers hurrying out of the backcountry.) You may encounter a rainy or snowy day during your visit. Make the most of it with the following activities.

- Tour the Alberta Visitor Center in West Glacier
- See the excellent Native American exhibits in the St. Mary Visitor Center
- Curl up with a book by the fireplace in Many Glacier Hotel or Lake McDonald Lodge
- Photograph the park during the rain or after a snowfall
- Watch the weather from a cozy rocking chair on the covered porch of Lake McDonald Lodge
- Play a board game or solve a jigsaw puzzle, always on hand in the common rooms at Many Glacier Hotel and Glacier Park Lodge
- Enjoy live music and entertainment at Many Glacier Hotel
- Dress for the weather and enjoy a stroll on a nature trail (see page 19)
- Experience High Tea at the Prince of Wales Hotel

BEST PLACES TO PHOTOGRAPH

A typical day in Glacier National Park is rich with photogenic surprises: wildlife encounters, scenic vistas, beautiful blossoms, spectacular lighting,

and wild weather. The list is endless. So keep your camera handy, and remember to look for small, close-up gems—the fringe on a wildflower's petals, the bright stain of lichen on rock—even when you're surrounded by vast, stunning mountain panoramas.

What are the iconic images of the park that you must photograph to remember your visit and to share with your friends and family? Here are the time-honored locations that should be included in every photo album.

- St. Mary Lake with Wild Goose Island from the Wild Goose Overlook

- St. Mary Lake and Logan Pass from the direction finder at Sun Point

- Logan Pass Continental Divide sign

- Mt. Reynolds with wildflower foreground, Logan Pass (you might get mountain goats or bighorn sheep in your picture)

- Haystack Butte and the Garden Wall from the Oberlin Bend turnout

- The Weeping Wall

- Any of the Glacier National Park entrance signs (Chief Highway from Alberta is the best. It is the only one to say Waterton-Glacier International Peace Park)

- Lunch Creek south of Going-to-the-Sun Road with the bridge in the foreground (cross your fingers for a Red Bus passing over the bridge)

- Lake McDonald from Apgar

- Two Medicine Lake (early morning, when the lake is mirror-like)
- Running Eagle Falls (mid-summer season to photograph water flowing over the precipice as well as from the cave)
- Many Glacier Hotel/Swiftcurrent Lake with mountain backdrop from the knoll east of the hotel
- Haystack Cascade
- The Prince of Wales Hotel

For a group photograph, or special portrait, the best places are:

- The park entrance stations. The most popular are West Glacier, St. Mary, and Many Glacier
- The Continental Divide sign at Logan Pass
- Wild Goose Island vista at St. Mary Lake
- The view of Lake McDonald from the Apgar Village shoreline
- Cameron Falls (Waterton)

NATURE'S ROCK ART

You will find lichens living in the alpine tundra, as well as in the valley floors and in every environment in between. Mountain goats rely on some varieties for sustenance, and northern flying squirrels get water by eating lichens hanging from trees. Varieties living on rocks display myriad colors, textures, and growth designs that may have been developing for a century. Look for nature's rock art as you walk the trails.

Photo by Sam Simpson.

BEST PLACES TO PEOPLE-WATCH

Visitors arrive from around the world to see Glacier National Park's scenery and wildlife. The excitement is infectious, especially where crowds gather. Two of the best places to watch people having the times of their lives are atop Logan Pass and amidst the Old World charm of the Many Glacier Hotel lobby.

Logan Pass

The Hidden Lake Trail from the Logan Pass Visitor Center to the Hidden Lake overlook is the best place to see large groups of people in various states of eager anticipation and astonishment. The exhilaration of alpine air and the appeal of the trail attract hundreds of visitors in July, August, and September. Numbers tend to peak at mid-day. Find a comfortable place to sit and watch the procession. Listen to the mixture of languages, and spot the excitement of fellow travelers. You may even see people with their snowboards or ski equipment hiking to the snowfields in July!

Many Glacier Hotel

Another hub of activity is in the lobby of the Many Glacier Hotel. Find a seat with a commanding view. See busloads of tourists showing their delight as they enter the rustic Swiss-style lodge for the first time. Watch visitors as they photograph the interior of the hotel, the panorama from the view windows, and the Bavarian-clad employees. Listen to returning hikers chattering above the sound of their bear bells. The best times to watch visitors are mid-morning, late afternoon, and early evening.

BEST PLACES TO READ A BOOK

After the sun goes down, or during inclement weather, even the most gung-ho hiker will welcome a chance to relax and enjoy the comforts of Waterton-Glacier International Peace Park's great indoors.

Many Glacier Hotel Lobby

Many Glacier Hotel's lobby is one of the most relaxing and entertaining indoor places in the park. Nestle in a chair close to the circular fireplace, find a spot close to the piano, or select a comfortable place at one of the view windows. The large, high-ceiling lobby lets you get lost unto yourself, even when there is a crowd.

◄ Lake McDonald Lodge

Select a rocking chair in front of the huge fireplace and settle in. The crackle of the fire in the setting of a hunting lodge makes this an ideal atmosphere to become absorbed in your book.

Prince of Wales Hotel Lobby ▾

The impressive floor-to-ceiling windows overlooking Upper Waterton Lake and the comfortable seating in the

hotel invite you to read. The best time to linger, listen to music, and read is during High Tea, daily from 2 p.m. to 4 p.m.

Chuck Haney Photography.

Best Books about Glacier

The following titles are as entertaining as they are informative. A good book can inspire you to further explore all the park has to offer.

Photography Books

 *Glacier Impressions*, John Reddy and Kerry Nickou

- *Glacier Unforgettable*, Chuck Haney
- *Mountain Goats of Glacier National Park*, Sumio Harada and Kathleen Yale

Good Reads

- *Glacier Country*, Bert Gildart and others
- *Glacier Day Hikes*, Alan Leftridge
- *Glacier's Historic Hotels & Chalets: View with a Room*, Ray Djuff and Chris Morrison
- *Glacier National Park: The First 100 Years*, C. W. Guthrie
- *Going-to-the-Sun Road: Glacier National Park's Highway to the Sky*, C. W. Guthrie
- *Great Lodges of the National Parks*, Christine Barnes
- *Pictures, a Park, and a Pulitzer*, Tom Lawrence
- *All Aboard for Glacier: The Great Northern Railway and Glacier National Park*, C.W. Guthrie
- *Glacier Park Lodge: Celebrating 100 Years*, Christine Barnes

Kids' Books

- *Glacier Babies*, Farcountry Press
- *Go Wild for Puzzles: Glacier National Park*, Robert Rath
- *Going to Glacier National Park*, Alan Leftridge
- *Who Pooped in the Park?* Gary Robson

BEST PLACES TO LISTEN TO LIVE MUSIC

Throughout the summer, Blackfeet visual and performing artists present music, poetry, and dance at several venues in Glacier. The "Native American Speaks" program affords visitors a deeper understanding of people's cultural attachment to the land. The programs offer the best live music in Glacier. You can enjoy performances at St. Mary Visitor Center, Many Glacier Hotel, and Lake McDonald Lodge. Look for the schedule in the park newspaper, and posted in campgrounds, visitor centers, and concessionaire establishments.

RESOURCES

The entries listed here are for informational purposes only; no endorsement or recommendation is intended or implied.

Glacier National Park
General Information
nps.gov/glac

Visitor Information
(406) 888-7806
(406) 888-7800 Telecommunication Device for the Deaf (TDD)

St. Mary Visitor Center
406-732-7750

Going-to-the-Sun Road Information
www.nps.gov/glac/planyourvisit/goingtothesunroad.htm

Campground Reservations
1-877-444-6777 or online at www.recreation.gov/

Fishing Regulations in Glacier
www.nps.gov/glac/planyourvisit/fishing
Fishing regulations can change any time. For the most recent regulations, talk with a ranger at any visitor center.

Bicycling in Glacier
www.nps.gov/glac/planyourvisit/bicycling.htm

Waterton Lakes National Park
General Information
www.pc.gc.ca/pn-np/ab/waterton/index.aspx
403-859-5133

Emergency
403-859-2636

Campground Reservations
www.pccamping.ca or 1-877-RESERVE (1-877-737-3783)

Glacier Park, Inc. Information and Reservations
glacierparkinc.com
In the U.S.: 406-892-2525
In Canada: 403-236-3400

Red Bus Reservations
406-892-2525

Boat Tours and Rentals
Glacier Park Boat Company
www.glacierparkboats.com
406-257-2426
Summer 406-888-5727; 406-732-4480; 406-732-4430

Waterton Shoreline Cruise Company
www.watertoncruise.com
403-859-2362

Horseback Rides in Glacier
The only licensed horseback rides in Glacier are conducted by Swan Mountain Outfitters.

Year-round reservations:
406-387-4405; toll-free 877-888-5557

Same-day reservations:
Apgar Corral: 406-888-5010
Lake McDonald Corral: 406-888-5121
Many Glacier Corral: 406-732-4203
West Glacier Corral: 406-387-5005

ABOUT THE AUTHOR

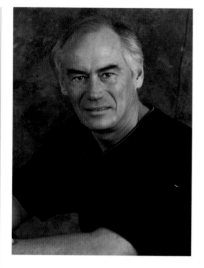

Alan Leftridge has served as a seasonal naturalist in Yellowstone National Park and a wilderness ranger in the Mission Mountains Wilderness. He earned a Bachelor of Science degree in biology at the University of Central Missouri, a secondary teaching credential from the University of Montana, and a Ph.D. in science education and cultural geography at Kansas State University. His career has included teaching high school science in West Yellowstone, science courses at Miami University, and environmental studies at Humboldt State University. Books to his credit include, Glacier Day Hikes, Seeley-Swan Day Hikes, Going to Glacier, *and* Interpretive Writing. *Alan lives south of Glacier National Park in the Swan Valley.*